Integrating
Teaching, Learning, and
Action Research

Integrating Teaching, Learning, and Action Research

Enhancing Instruction in the K–12 Classroom

Ernest T. Stringer
Curtin University of Technology

Lois McFadyen Christensen
University of Alabama at Birmingham

Shelia C. Baldwin
Monmouth University

Los Angeles | London | New Delhi
Singapore | Washington DC

For information:

SAGE Publications, Inc.
2455 Teller Road
Thousand Oaks, California 91320
E-mail: order@sagepub.com

SAGE Publications Ltd.
1 Oliver's Yard
55 City Road
London EC1Y 1SP
United Kingdom

SAGE Publications India Pvt. Ltd.
B 1/I 1 Mohan Cooperative Industrial Area
Mathura Road, New Delhi 110 044
India

SAGE Publications Asia-Pacific Pte. Ltd.
33 Pekin Street #02-01
Far East Square
Singapore 048763

Printed in the United States of America

Library of Congress Cataloging-in-Publication Data

Stringer, Ernest T.
Integrating teaching, learning, and action research: enhancing instruction in the K–12 classroom/Ernest T. Stringer, Lois McFadyen Christensen, Shelia C. Baldwin.
    p. cm.
Includes bibliographical references and index.
ISBN 978-1-4129-3975-1 (pbk.)

    1. Action research in education. 2. Teaching. I. Christensen, Lois McFadyen. II. Baldwin, Shelia C. III. Title.

LB1028.24.S87 2009
370.72—dc22   2008041302

This book is printed on acid-free paper.

09 10 11 12 13 10 9 8 7 6 5 4 3 2 1

Acquisitions Editor:	Diane McDaniel
Editorial Assistants:	Ashley Conlon, Leah Mori
Production Editor:	Brittany Bauhaus
Copy Editor:	Teresa Wilson
Typesetter:	C&M Digitals (P) Ltd.
Proofreader:	Jenifer Kooiman
Indexer:	Diggs Publication Services
Cover Designer:	Bryan Fishman
Marketing Manager:	Christy Guilbault

Brief Contents

Detailed Contents

Appendix. Case Examples   141

Preface

The past century has seen wonderful developments in education, so that schools are now much more humane and child-friendly places than they once were. They provide a curriculum that is more focused on the needs of student and community, and use diverse approaches to learning that contrast markedly to the arcane and rigid classrooms common in past eras. Schools are much more student centered, and teachers gain great satisfaction from the contribution they are able to make to the intellectual, emotional, and social development of their students.

A range of reports have pointed to the need, however, for schools to keep pace with the dramatic developments now sweeping the world. Not only is the landscape of social life changing, but also education has the challenge of preparing children for workplaces where knowledge and skills rapidly become outmoded. The need for people who are self-directing, lifelong learners is becoming increasingly evident. The focus on broad-ranging educational outcomes emerges from the need for a well-informed citizenry that is able to thrive in changing environments.

Despite this, however, schools are still hampered by outmoded practices, now acknowledged to be of limited educational benefit, that are still prevalent in many classrooms. Teacher presentation and student recall are still the method of choice for many teachers, despite the now wide range of exciting possibilities that have the potential to enrich the educational experience of students and provide teachers with greater levels of professional and personal satisfaction.

THE PURPOSE OF THE BOOK

This text is based on the intention to integrate elements of instruction that emerged in the latter decades of the 20th century. We present teaching not as a mechanistic, unthinking, technical process, but as a creative, reflective process that taps into the talents and potentials of every student, actively involving them in processes of learning that engage their full educational potential.

At the heart of the approach to instruction and learning we present is an *attitude of inquiry* that permeates all classroom activities for both teacher and student. This attitude of inquiry provides the basis for the teacher to plan, implement, and evaluate lessons. It also permeates the learning process incorporated into classroom lessons, processes of inquiry and exploration providing the means for students to accomplish the full range of standards now recognized in curricula everywhere.

The frameworks of teaching and learning that follow, therefore, incorporate the most significant features of recent educational development that will lead us into this emerging millennium. We demonstrate how recent developments in action research provide a framework for teaching and learning that can be integrated into both direct instruction and inquiry learning. Our hope is that these processes will provide students with a more creative, rigorous, and developmental education that enables them to accomplish a more productive and harmonious life in their families, communities, and workplaces.

Example lesson plans included throughout the book are derived from state standards in Alabama and New Jersey. These standards are associated with specific states; however, most state standards are drawn from U.S. national state standards that, though they differ in detail, follow very similar formats. Other minor differences in format in the example lesson plans emerge from differences in requirements of different school districts, though all cover the same essential elements of a lesson.

STRUCTURE OF THE BOOK

Chapter 1 presents a simple, cyclical action research process comprising three basic elements:

Look	Gathering information
Think	Analysis of that information
Act	Using the outcomes of analysis to take some action

This process is applied throughout the book, and following chapters show how this simple routine guides activity in each phase of instruction—lesson planning, instruction (teaching), and assessment. Chapter 1 also indicates that student action research (or action learning) is a parallel process, teachers engaging in processes of inquiry in tandem with their students to track the progress of learning throughout lessons.

Chapter 2 presents the theoretical underpinnings of this approach to instruction. It clearly describes a variety of theories of education, learning, and development that point to the need for systematic processes of inquiry that lie at the heart of this approach to instruction and learning.

Chapter 3 presents the first phase of instruction—lesson planning. It demonstrates how the Look–Think–Act action research routine assists teachers to systematically investigate all elements that need to be taken into account to construct effective and comprehensive lesson plans. These include not only student capabilities and characteristics, but also the elements of instruction to be incorporated. The chapter provides case studies that show how this process can be applied within both direct instruction and inquiry learning approaches to teaching and learning.

Chapter 4 first delineates the conditions that teachers need to take into account to ensure effective instruction and learning processes—student engagement and student prior knowledge. It also describes the different forms of knowledge that provide the basis for a comprehensive education, describing the taxonomies of educational objectives that form the basis for many curricula. It then presents the second phase of instruction—initiating and facilitating student learning activities, showing how action research routines assist the teacher to systematically observe and analyze student learning processes.

Chapter 5 switches focus from teacher to student, and shows student learning processes working in tandem with teachers' instructional processes. Using the same framework inquiry, termed an *action learning process*, students systematically acquire information, engage in processes of analysis and synthesis, and make tangible use of the outcomes of their inquiries to demonstrate proficiency in desired learning outcomes.

Chapter 6 demonstrates how the Look–Think–Act process of inquiry assists teachers and students to systematically assess student learning and evaluate the outcomes of lessons. The chapter first describes the genesis of the current focus on state and national outcomes, and then describes how action research routines, through a variety of assessment rubrics, ensure that student performances are linked directly to lesson objectives and state outcome statements.

Finally, the **Appendix** presents three exemplary lessons that demonstrate the way processes of inquiry have been effectively applied to complex, but highly effective, lessons.

Authors' Note: The authors wish to acknowledge that the order in which their names appear does not indicate the respective worth of their contributions to this text.

Acknowledgments

We would like to gratefully acknowledge the valuable material provided by the teachers whose lesson plans are included in each of the chapters. These are testament to the dedication and skill of educators who, like many of their colleagues, work tirelessly to provide for the educational needs of their students. Through their work we have been able to ground the frameworks of action research in the real world of teaching practice and to present a resource that resonates with the realities of daily life in classrooms and schools. We therefore would like to thank Cameron McKinley, Laurie Drennen Noblitt, Ellen Stubblefield, Deanna Iorio, and Eric Wasnesky for their wonderful contributions to this book.

Writing this text has required an extended process of development, entailing careful thought and much patience as we worked our way through the many iterations needed to bring it to fruition. We are heartily grateful to our spouses—Rosalie Dwyer, John Baldwin, and Paul Christensen—for their wonderful support during some of the more demanding times in our journey. The hospitality and friendship they provided were truly supportive and inspirational, and we thank them from the bottom of our hearts.

We would also like to acknowledge the patient and systematic support provided by the staff at SAGE. Through their efforts, this book has become a much more accessible text that more clearly provides readers with the tools to engage their teaching practices. We particularly recognize the assistance and support of our acquisitions editor, Diane McDaniel, and editorial assistants, Leah Mori and Ashley Conlon.

The authors and SAGE gratefully acknowledge the contributions of the following reviewers:

Mary Frances Agnello, *Texas Tech University*

Sue Boldra, *Fort Hays State University*

Mary D. Burbank, *University of Utah*

Brec Cooke, *American University*

Kisha N. Daniels, *North Carolina Central University*

Jennifer Esposito, *Georgia State University*

Marina Gair, *Pace University*

Patricia M. McCollum, *Piedmont College*

D. John McIntyre, *Southern Illinois University Carbondale*

Suzanne Medina, *California State University, Dominguez Hills*

Lisa Downing Murley, *Western Kentucky University*

Linda Donica Payne, *East Tennessee State University*

Robert J. Redmon, *Midwestern State University*

Margaret Riel, *Pepperdine University*

Gail Singleton Taylor, *Old Dominion University*

Beth N. Tope, *Louisiana State University*

Frances van Tassell, *University of North Texas*

Camille M. Yates, *Southeastern Louisiana University*

Action Research in Teaching and Learning

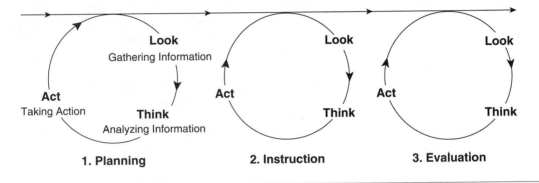

Action Research in Phases of Teaching

This chapter shows how *action research* can be used to *enhance the craft of teaching* by assisting teachers to organize and facilitate effective programs of student learning.

It describes how action research can assist teachers to take into account the *characteristics and abilities* of their students—intelligences, personalities, emotional states, stages of development, and family backgrounds.

Action research is presented as a *cyclical, repetitive process of inquiry* that guides teacher preparation and instruction:

Look: Gathering information

Think: Reflecting on, or analyzing, the information

Act: Planning, implementing, and evaluating student learning

Action learning is presented as a similar process of inquiry that guides student learning—Look, Think, Act.

1

Action research and action learning *are parallel processes* that enable teacher and student to work in tandem to accomplish effective learning processes.

The chapter then briefly describes how action research can be applied to three phases of instruction—*planning, instruction, and evaluation.*

MYSELF AS TEACHER: THE REFLECTIVE PRACTITIONER

As a classroom teacher I would start the school year thinking about the classroom that was to emerge in the coming weeks—the students that would come to me, and the task of teaching them. Who are the children? What will they be like? What will they need to learn? How will I plan and organize the learning that my students must accomplish? There would be so much to do! Although initially a little daunted by the task, my professional preparation and experience provided the set of resources with which to systematically construct a syllabus and organize my classroom so that I was ready for the arrival of my students.

The students would arrive in class on the first day of school eager to see what their teacher had in store for them. For the more able, excitement and expectation at the possibilities of engaging in interesting and rewarding activities fed the positive experience they expected from school. Others were more wary, conscious of the sometimes precarious demands that are made of them, and the possibility of embarrassment or feelings of inadequacy that accompany them as they enter the classroom.

As I gained experience, I became more aware of the many dimensions of my students that I had to take into account as I planned lessons for my class. They often came from quite diverse backgrounds, the racial, ethnic, and national diversity evident in their dress, behaviors, interests, attitudes, and responses. These, in turn, were clearly influenced by their family circumstances, the television shows they watched, the type of parenting they had received, and the quality of their community life, as well as their individual dispositions and abilities, and their relationships with their peers.

But I also learned that I couldn't take anything for granted, and that often my "eyeballing" of students could lead to quite mistaken conclusions. I remember "Max," whose slouched body and scruffy clothes, together with a rather sullen appearance, masked a little "gem." Although initially somewhat reticent, he could transform the class with insightful, witty, and ultimately informative remarks, and his knowledge of the inner workings of a computer became legendary in the class.

As I built my understanding of my students, I became increasingly sensitive to their different needs, capabilities, and attitudes and the creative teaching strategies I could employ to engage them in learning activities that not only held their attention but, in the best of times, excited them greatly. Becoming frustrated with the tired response of one class to the social studies program I had planned, I gave them their head and asked them to explore a topic of their own choosing, asking only that they provide an interesting presentation to the class that used a variety of media. The outcomes were quite spectacular, resulting in a parents night in which students proudly presented their projects to an assembled group of family members.

As I reflect on my work with students, therefore, I am reminded that teaching, such a rewarding profession when done well, requires me to engage all aspects of my professional self—my head, my heart, and my hands. To do it well, I need to quite consciously employ reflective processes of inquiry that enable me to answer the questions in the first paragraph of this section. I now see this reflective process as action research—a process of systematic inquiry that provides a clearly defined body of concepts and ideas with which I can accomplish the wonderful art and craft of teaching.

—E.S.

THE CRAFT OF TEACHING: ORGANIZING AND FACILITATING STUDENT LEARNING

Common views of teaching see it as a relatively straightforward process, selected content being organized into a lesson plan that sets out the sequence of activities required to accomplish student learning objectives and outcomes. Preservice teachers soon learn that there is much more involved, however, and learn to accomplish the rather complex task of preparing a lesson plan. Typically, this will incorporate:

Objectives/Outcomes: What students will know and be able to do by the end of the lesson

Standards: State requirements for student learning

Procedures: A sequence of learning activities

Assessment: Tasks that demonstrate student levels of performance on each of the standards

Materials: Materials and equipment required during the lesson

Teachers commonly encompass lesson plans within a grid or table (see Figure 1.1) that enables them to check the progress of the lesson as students move through the sets of learning activities and assessment tasks.

Grade Level:			
Subject:			
Unit Title/Lesson Title:			
Key Standards:			
Time/Duration:			
Special Needs and ELL Modifications:			
Materials			
Objectives/Outcomes & Standards	**Teacher Procedures**	**Student Procedures**	**Assessment**

Figure 1.1   A Typical Lesson Planning Grid

A well-planned and -executed lesson provides both teachers and students with high degrees of satisfaction, and is the basis for a successful and rewarding classroom experience. As we highlight below, however, the ability of teachers to accomplish these professionally desirable outcomes requires them to take into account the many facets of children and learning that comprise the art of teaching. Teaching is not just a mechanical process of presenting lessons and testing students, but a real craft that requires systematic and creative work to achieve the educational outcomes required of the diverse students that face teachers in their classrooms. Further, it is a social production that requires teachers to consciously build a learning community that nurtures children and enables them to work together in highly productive ways.

THE COMPLEXITIES OF TEACHING AND LEARNING

Planning a lesson is more than just setting out a program of learning, however. A teacher must take into account not only the information or skills to be learned, but also the characteristics and capabilities of the students in the class. A successful program of learning requires careful alignment of what is to be learned with the qualities of the learner.

STUDENT CHARACTERISTICS AND CAPABILITIES

Think of the different classrooms in which you have taught or which you have visited. Students in a typical classroom come from a broad range of family and community backgrounds. Some may come from very traditional families comprised of mother, father, and children. Many children, however, may live in single-parent families lacking either a father or a mother, may be part of a blended family with children from two previous families, may have parents of the same sex, may live with relatives, or may be housed in a foster home. In some high schools, students may be self-supporting, or have responsibilities for caring for their siblings. Any of these situations may vary in the degree to which they provide an environment in which children can grow and develop. Some may be stable and nurturing, the children experiencing lives that are generally harmonious and organized, while others may live in homes where parents are often in conflict, or where the dysfunctional relationships are not conducive to the experience of a happy childhood.

But differences in experience go even deeper, as some children will be raised in contexts where the parents are fully employed with adequate incomes that enable them to provide for the everyday needs of their children. Others will experience families that struggle almost from day to day to make adequate provision for food, dress, and housing. Aligned with these differences are differences in employment that characterize the broad cross-section of any society, from unskilled workers in service industries, through tradespeople, clerical, professional, and business and industry. Parental occupations provide a broad range of differences in lifestyle, aspirations, attitudes, values and behaviors, and social orientations (e.g., see the box "Occupational Preferences").

OCCUPATIONAL PREFERENCES

When I was a teenager, my father, a working-class man, used his social contacts to arrange a clerical job for me. From his perspective, this was a "plum" occupation that would set me up for life, and he was totally surprised when I rejected his offer, indicating that I wished to continue my schooling and become a teacher. Teaching, to him, who had left school very early, was a mysterious job that seemed outside the reach of his son. It was only by strenuous argument that he allowed me, somewhat begrudgingly, to take up a path that seemed, from his perspective, to lack the promise so evident in the clerical position he had arranged. Despite my later success in my chosen occupation, he never really understood or accepted the wisdom of my choice, and I never felt that I had, in his eyes, been successful.

—E.S.

But differences in experience and orientation go even deeper than this. The racial and ethnic diversity that is part of almost any neighborhood in today's modern society means that children will come from families that have deep-seated differences in attitudes, behaviors, and outlooks. These differences are not always evident, but have the potential to greatly affect children's learning. Teachers need to provide learning activities that not only take account of these cultural characteristics, but take advantage of them to enhance the learning environment of their classroom community.

Children from these different contexts, therefore, come to school with a variety of behaviors and responses that derive from their family and community experiences. The differences, however, go even deeper, since children will also differ in their behaviors and responses according to the individual characteristics that are part of their genetic inheritance. Some will have abilities that enable them to easily accomplish the academic tasks that are part of school life, while others will struggle with the complexities of the written word and the intricacies of numbers. Some will have keen eyesight, or good hand–eye coordination, while others are near- or farsighted, and struggle with the small physical tasks—writing, drawing, cutting, throwing, catching, and so on—that are part of regular classroom and school activity. Students will also differ in their emotional makeup, their growth and development, and their ability to interact with others. Many classrooms contain children whose degree of difference—emotional, physical, intellectual, language—is so marked that they require particular attention to accommodate their special needs.

Any classroom, therefore, is a veritable "zoo" of abilities, orientations, responses, behaviors, and potentials. The students comprise a diverse body of individuals whose characteristics and qualities need to be taken into account as teachers strive to provide an effective and enjoyable education for the children in their charge. The excitement of teaching is grounded in the rich potential encompassed by the students, the bubbling energy that is nascent in any group of young people, and the task of providing them with learning experiences that "make a difference" in their lives. A teacher's main task is to construct an ongoing set of learning experiences that not only provide students with the knowledge and skills that enhance their understanding of the social world in which they live, but provide them with skills they will need to live happy and productive lives in a complex, modern society.

WHAT IS TO BE LEARNED: DOMAINS OF KNOWLEDGE

The teaching task is also made more complex by the wide array of knowledge and skills that comprise the curriculum. The purpose of schooling is to pass on to students that vast body of knowledge that is the accumulated wisdom of modern societies, and is the product of many centuries of development and learning. Some people act as if "learning" this body of knowledge is merely an act of memorization and retrieval—remembering pieces of knowledge and retrieving them in response to appropriate questions—or applying a memorized formula to acquire a correct answer. From this perspective, the major tasks involved in learning are presentation and recall.

"Knowing," however, entails much more than merely being able to remember a specific piece of knowledge. Knowing, at a deeper level, entails the ability to use that knowledge in a range of different ways; knowing is related to "understanding." Understanding indicates the ability a person acquires to creatively apply and use that piece of knowledge—to extrapolate from it, to link it to other discrete pieces of information, to use it to solve problems, and so on. These different domains of knowledge have been clearly articulated by Benjamin Bloom and his colleagues (Bloom & Krathwohl, 1956), whose Taxonomy of Educational Objectives has for many years provided a useful way to conceptualize the different forms of knowing, enabling us to understand how human learning is not merely a process of memorization, but entails a number of different types or *domains* of knowledge:

- **Knowledge:** Remembering and being able to recall information
- **Comprehension:** Grasping the meaning of informational materials
- **Application:** Using that information in new situations
- **Analysis:** Breaking down information into component parts, developing divergent conclusions, making inferences, and finding evidence to support arguments

- **Synthesis:** Applying prior knowledge and skills to produce a new arrangement of the knowledge

- **Evaluation:** Judging the value of a product

These cognitive skills form the basis for much of our educational endeavors, so that as students move through school, they extend their capacity to engage these types of activity. Their knowledge increases in breadth, and they become increasingly adept at performing more complex cognitive tasks. The above taxonomy emphasizes cognitive or intellectual functioning, but equivalent taxonomies describe knowledge in the affective domain (feeling and emotion) and the psychomotor domain (motor skills). As teachers plan and implement their lessons, therefore, they need to keep track of the multitude of learning tasks required to accomplish a very diverse set of learning outcomes.

The purpose of incorporating action research routines into teaching, therefore, is to provide teachers with a framework or scaffold that enables them to systematically take into account these diverse issues. Action research as a simple process of systematic inquiry provides the means by which teachers can organize the complexity they face and assists them to incorporate the diverse elements of instruction into a carefully articulated program of learning for their students.

ACTION RESEARCH IN TEACHING

Although teaching is often viewed as the simple procedure of presenting students with a body of subject matter that is learned and tested, experienced teachers know that much more is involved. They understand the need to take into account the diverse abilities and characteristics of their students, the complex body of knowledge and skills that students must acquire, and the diverse learning activities that need to be engaged. In many respects, also, each class is different from any other, and requires a carefully planned program of activities to ensure that students achieve successful learning outcomes. Action research provides the means for teachers to incorporate these diverse elements into their instruction, and to organize their work so that they effectively accomplish the demanding task of teaching.

There is nothing magical or particularly complex about action research. It is merely a systematic routine that enables teachers to keep track and take account of the many aspects of their work with students. Action research is similar to steps we take as we investigate very ordinary problems and issues in our everyday life. If we can't find our socks, we might first "Look" for them, or even ask our partners, "Have you seen my blue socks?" We then "Think" about them, asking questions like, "Where did I put them?" "When did I last use them?" "Did I put them in the wash?"

thereby examining alternative explanations for their possible location. If we are successful in these activities, the final "Act" is to find the socks, and the problem is solved.

In a similar vein, action research enables teachers to answer the basic instructional questions described above. The fundamental research question, however, can be stated as "How can I provide a successful lesson for this particular group of students?" As we reveal in the coming chapters, this question requires teachers to engage in systematic inquiry that enables us to take into account the many issues that are part of any classroom learning process—the nature of our students, the outcomes to be achieved, the content to be learned, the learning activities involved, and the means for assessing that learning.

The approach to action research as applied to teaching in this book is based on a simple LOOK > THINK > ACT heuristic[1] that frames both the instructional work of the teacher and student learning activities. The three components act as a compass or map that guides teachers through the systematic steps of a process of inquiry:

LOOK   Acquire information (data)

THINK   Reflect on the information (analyze)

ACT   Use outcomes of reflection and analysis (plan, implement, evaluate)

This simple process is repeated in an ongoing fashion, providing a constant guide to ongoing processes of teaching and learning (Figure 1.2).

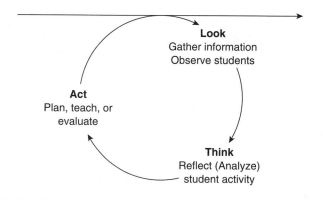

Figure 1.2   Action Research Cycle

Action research is often used to investigate specific issues or problems associated with classroom or school life (Atweh & Burton, 1995; Atweh, Christensen, & Dornan, 1998; Baldwin, 1996; Kincheloe, 2005; Malaguzzi, 1994; Stringer 2008). In this text, however, we show it may be continuously applied to ongoing classroom teaching and learning routines. Action research therefore becomes an integral part of classroom lessons, providing a scaffold on which to build creative and effective lessons that consciously engage the students' full learning potential. It assists teachers to link student learning to real-life contexts, interests, and experiences, and provides an approach to experiential education that boosts student learning while promoting social outcomes related to participatory democracy.

ACTION LEARNING FOR STUDENTS

This book is based on the assumption that students learn more and better when they are actively engaged in processes of inquiry that stimulate their imagination and their interest. Action learning envisions learning, like action research, as a systematic process of inquiry and investigation that encompasses a wide range of interesting and effective learning activities. Action learners are, in effect, action researchers, as will become apparent in the following sections.

When teachers ask students to "research a topic and write a paper," they are asking them to gather information and report on a topic or issue. Students typically use a variety of methods to acquire information from a variety of sources—books, magazines, papers, the Internet, television, and so on. From all they gather, they select interesting or relevant pieces of information to construct their report that summarizes the central concepts, issues, and events and presents them in a carefully organized form. A good report provides readers with a clear understanding of the topic or issue studied.

This common event encapsulates some fundamental features of the processes of investigation that is the hallmark of scientific, social, and behavioral research. Using processes of investigation that are similar to those used in these types of research, students explore a topic or issue by conducting systematic processes of inquiry that

- **Focus:** Clarify the issue, topic, or problem to be studied

- **Gather Data:** Collect information relevant to that issue, topic, or problem

- **Analyze Data:** Process that information by selecting and sorting to identify key elements

- **Action:** Perform some action or activity that uses the information thus acquired

Action learners move through continuous cycles of this inquiry process to improve their understanding, extend their knowledge, or refine their skills (see Figure 1.3).

Action learning enables students to apply active learning processes to any area of the curriculum—reading, writing, mathematics, social studies, science, and so on. In the following pages we demonstrate how student action learning activities are clearly linked to outcomes embodied in state courses of study or core content curricula standards.

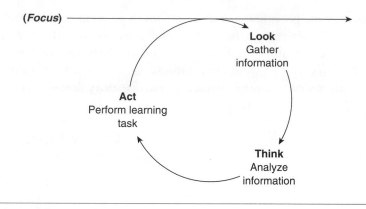

Figure 1.3   Action Learning Cycle

ACTION RESEARCH AND ACTION LEARNING: PARALLEL PROCESSES

The above frameworks describe how action research—a process of systematic inquiry—assists teachers to formulate lessons and evaluate the outcomes of the learning processes they contain. It enables teachers to systematically sort through the range of issues they need to accommodate in their lessons in order to accomplish effective outcomes with their students. A process of inquiry requires a teacher to start with questions about their students:

- What are the characteristics and qualities of the students I am teaching?

- What must they learn?

- How can they learn it?

- How can I know the extent to which they have learned it?

These are *research questions* that provide the basis for a continuing process of exploration that enables a teacher to plan effective classroom learning strategies. As these lessons are implemented, he or she monitors student progress using ongoing cycles of the action research process, observing student activities, assessing student performance, and providing appropriate feedback (see "Teacher" column in Figure 1.4).

A similar process of inquiry—action learning—assists students to frame their activities in terms of a series of questions. Starting with a topic, an issue, or a problem that focuses on a particular body of knowledge or set of concepts and/or skills, they may ask:

- What do I need to learn? What do I need to *know* or to be able to *do*?

- How can I learn those things?

- How can I show that I have learned them?

Action Research		**Action Learning**
The Teacher		**Students**
Looks **(Gathers information)** Observes student learning activity	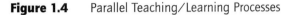	**Look** **(Gather information)** Acquire information by looking, listening, and doing
Thinks **(Reflects, analyzes)** Assesses student performance	←————————→	**Think** **(Reflect, analyze)** Process information— remembering, selecting, organizing
Acts **(Takes action)** Provides students with feedback	←————————→	**Act** **(Take action)** Perform an activity to demonstrate their understanding or competence

Figure 1.4   Parallel Teaching/Learning Processes

The learning processes that merge exploration of these questions provide the means to assist students to more effectively accomplish the outcomes that are the purpose of the lesson (see the column for "Students" in Figure 1.4).

Teachers and students are therefore engaged in parallel processes of inquiry that enable students to accomplish their learning, and assist teachers to engage more effective teaching practices. As Figure 1.5 indicates, the teacher's reflective research routine mirrors the learning routine of students, providing the context for creative and engaged instruction and learning.

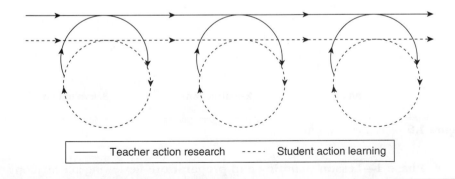

Teacher action research   - - - - -   Student action learning

Figure 1.5   Action Research/Action Learning Double Helix

The following chapters therefore describe how action research and action learning work in tandem to provide students and teachers with the means to implement an approach to learning that is dynamic, engaging, and educationally effective. In a fundamental way teaching and learning, as a transactional process, require both teachers and students to engage in ongoing acts of systematic inquiry that enable them to successfully accomplish learning outcomes that are the true purpose of classroom life.

The relationship between teaching and learning can be envisaged as a double helix, the parallel processes of teacher instruction and student learning working as complementary parts of the same process. In the following chapters we describe how these interacting spirals of activity provide a framework of concepts upon which to scaffold teaching and learning to produce enhanced outcomes in the classroom.

APPLYING ACTION RESEARCH TO PHASES OF INSTRUCTION

As described above, action research is not an "add-on" to the regular work of teaching but a set of procedures or a scaffold—a structured way of thinking—that assists teachers to engage their regular teaching routines in a more systematic and organized fashion. A lesson plan, for instance, is presented not merely as a standardized recipe for instruction, but the product of systematic inquiry that assists the teacher to deal with the complex array of issues that must be taken into account in planning and implementing effective teaching/learning processes.

Action research is not just applied to lesson planning, however, but can be incorporated into all aspects of teaching. The chapters that follow describe how to use action research to enhance each phase of instruction—planning, teaching, and assessment and evaluation (see Figure 1.6):

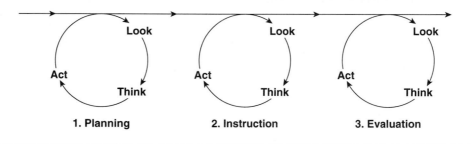

Figure 1.6   Phases of Instruction

- **Phase 1—Lesson planning and preparation:** Reviewing information and resources (Look); selecting, sorting, and organizing information (Think); formulating a lesson plan (Act).

- **Phase 2—Instruction:** Initiating activity and observing student responses (Look); reflecting on their learning processes and performances (Think); providing feedback and information (Act).

- **Phase 3—Assessment and Evaluation:** Reviewing lesson outcomes, reviewing student performance (Look); identifying successes and strengths; identifying weaknesses and gaps (Think); Planning remedial actions; planning ways of improving instruction and learning (Act).

The cyclical Look–Think–Act steps of action research thus are incorporated into each phase of instruction, providing carefully articulated processes that enhance both teacher instruction and student learning.

CONCLUSION

This chapter has described how action research and action learning can enhance teacher instruction and student learning. It shows how systematic processes of inquiry can assist teachers to learn more about the fundamental attributes and capacities of their students, and use that information to enrich and enhance the teaching/learning processes in their classrooms. In doing so, teachers are able to take into account some of the fundamental conditions that enable students to engage the full potential of their learning capacities and capabilities. The following chapters provide detailed descriptions of how action research can provide the basis for incorporating this complex array of issues into each phase of the teaching process—planning, implementing, and evaluating lessons.

LEARNING RESOURCES

Reflection

1. **Look:**   Review the material on action research in this chapter.

   Think: Identify the major features of action research.

   Act: Prepare a short presentation that describes the way you understand action research. Present it to some of your colleagues or classmates.

2. **Look**:   Review the material in this chapter on action learning.

   Think: Identify the major features of action research. Identify how it is similar, and how it differs from action research.

   Act: Plan a short presentation on your findings to a small group of colleagues or classmates.

3. **Look**:   Review material in this chapter that describes how teachers can enhance their instruction by the use of action research.

   Think: Identify the framework(s) presented that you feel would be most useful to you, as a teacher.

   Act: Plan and implement a short presentation that describes these frameworks to a group of colleagues or classmates.

Web Sites

Action Research Resources:

www.scu.edu.au/schools/gcm/ar/arhome.html

>   The site provides an online journal, access to an online course, useful papers, and other general resources.

Jack Whitehead's Home Page:

www2.bath.ac.uk/~edsajw/home.html

>   Offers a wide range of resources to schools and education. Information includes many examples of action research projects, and links to other home pages.

Research for Action (RFA):

www.researchforaction.org/index.html

>   Educational research and reform to improve educational opportunities and outcomes for all students. A rich range of resources.

Action Research at Queen's University:

http://educ.queensu.ca/~ar

>   Links to programs, conferences, sites, resources, publications, and student and faculty reports related to action research.

A Beginner's Guide to Action Research:

http://ousd.k12.ca.us/netday/links/Action_Research/begin_guide_action_research

>   A very useful and comprehensive guide to action research from Bob Dick.

Classroom Action Research Overview:

www.iusb.edu/~gmetteta/Classroom_Action_Research.html

>   Assists the teacher to find out what's happening in her or his classroom.

Additional Reading

Holly, M., Ahar, J., & Kasten, W. (2004). *Action research for teachers: Traveling the yellow brick road* (2nd ed.). Upper Saddle River, NJ: Pearson.

McNiff, J., & Whitehead, J. (2006). *Action research for teachers: A practical guide*. Abingdon, UK: David Fulton Publishers.

Mills, G. (2007). *Action research: A guide for the teacher researcher* (3rd ed.). Upper Saddle River, NJ: Pearson.

Stringer, E. (2007). *Action research* (3rd ed.). Thousand Oaks, CA: Sage.

Stringer, E. (2008). *Action research in education* (2nd ed.). Upper Saddle River, NJ: Pearson.

NOTE

1. As a heuristic, the words are not meant as literal translations of the term, but merely signal a phase of exploration. The Look phase, for instance, may entail observation, listening, reading, and so on. Think may signal processes of reflection, remembering, analysis, sorting and selecting, and so on. The important issue is to focus on the intent of the process, as signaled by the terms. They are merely devices that act as signposts to keep us on track and clarify the nature of each type of activity.

Learning Theory

T he purpose of this chapter is to provide greater understanding of the complexity of student learning processes. It signals the wide range of factors teachers must take into account in their classroom teaching. Insights are drawn from the following theoretical perspectives:

- Cognitive and developmental theories that focus on
    - Ways information is processed, learned, and transferred
    - Learner adaptation
    - Stages of development of knowledge dispositions (Piaget)
    - Social learning theory (Vygotsky)
    - Inquiry, problem solving, and discovery that change learner cognitive structures (Bruner)
    - Multiple intelligences through which humans process information (Gardner)
    - Brain theory and its focus on biological propensity (Caine and Caine)

- Social learning theory that focuses on social imitation and observation (Bandura)
- Inquiry learning that focuses on learning through problem solving within the social world of the learner (Dewey)
- Postmodern perspectives that highlight the need to take into account the systems of meaning—social, cultural, and political—through which learners make sense of their environment
- Critical theory that shows how
    - Knowledge and understanding based on a teacher's history of experience is imposed on students in disempowering ways
    - Teachers need to take advantage of the cultural capital of the learner (Freire)
    - Democracy and social justice are learned in classrooms

Each of these theoretical perspectives suggests the need for teachers to approach the act of teaching as a process of inquiry to enhance their professional lives and provide greater satisfaction for their students.

MS. McKINLEY'S SOCIAL STUDIES LESSON

Ms. McKinley walked down the hill from the middle school to the assisted living care center to set up e-mail accounts so that her sixth graders could communicate with the elders there (LOOK). The sixth graders created Web pages about themselves so the residents could get to know them. They included interview questions about their histories in terms of family and so on. The residents e-mailed back and included photographs of family members and themselves, some of the benchmarks in their lives, significant historical occurrences, favorite music, service interests, military service if pertinent, and other areas of relevant information (ACT). Prior to the interviews, the sixth-grade students brainstormed interview questions; some questions were grand tour questions and others were mini-tour questions (THINK) (Spradley, 1980).

Once they gathered all of the information from the elders that they thought they needed, the difficult work began (LOOK). Each sixth grader developed a Web site for his or her particular elder (THINK). All of the students created hotlinks to the elders' favorite music from various eras throughout their lives. The students scanned in photographs and wrote some humorous and serious commentary for each. The elders' Web pages featured the particular person on the front page from digital photos taken at the center. Favorite music of each elder played throughout some of the students' entire presentation. Other students spent more time on backgrounds and fonts. Newspaper articles were researched and copied into some of the Web sites to make "exclamation points" about some of the assisted living residents' comments.

As the completion of the project drew near, Ms. McKinley invited the elders to come to the middle school one afternoon for a visit (ACT). Excitement filled the air in halls. Shortly after the last school bell rang, the short bus from the center pulled up in front of the main entrance to the school and the group of elders carefully exited with their chaperones. Soon everyone was reunited in Ms. McKinley's classroom, each elder with each student interviewer. The sixth graders were so pleased about premiering their Web sites. Some of the elders laughed in delight. Others cried with pride looking back over their past as the students presented the Web pages and clicked on the links revealing photographs of their family members or themselves as younger individuals. Music from eras gone by filled the room. The projects were viewed over and over again. All the while, Ms. McKinley captured the interaction through digital photographs. Neither the elders nor the sixth graders will ever forget this relational project where their work and learning made a difference in another's life.

Throughout these activities she knew she was providing her students with a rich and extensive set of learning activities that would provide for the full cognitive, social, emotional, and physical development of her students. As she worked with her children, she considered the theories she had learned in college and realized the meaningfulness of these perspectives to her teaching.

—L.C.

Chapter 1 signaled the diverse influences that affect learning, indicating that individual differences in personality and capability are reinforced and amplified by the effect of a student's home, community, and cultural background. This chapter is designed to provide a straightforward account of some of the theories that shed light on the factors affecting classroom teaching and learning. The extent to which teachers take into account these influences will determine the effectiveness of their instruction, and the learning outcomes achieved by their students. The integration of the Look–Think–Act process of inquiry into teaching provides the means to ensure that we systematically take these influences into account as we engage processes of instruction and learning.

A wide range of literature, the result of many years of research, indicates the nature and extent of these influences. Theories from the human sciences, particularly, provide the means to understand more clearly the complexity of the learning process, and explain why a "one size fits all" approach to education is unlikely to succeed. The different explanatory "lenses" of social and behavioral theory provide insights into the features of students and classroom life that provide the means for teachers to build, over time, a truly effective body of professional knowledge.

None of the theories is "right" or "wrong" in any fundamental sense, but each has an influence that affects student learning and behavior. Having an amalgamation of well-grounded theoretical tools enables educators at every level to adapt practice and be able to thoroughly express why a particular theory fits practice and is implemented and assessed. This knowledge-in-practice (Schon, 1983) type of "tool kit" enhances effective learning by all involved, including the teacher.

The following theoretical "snapshots" describe some of the fundamental elements of teaching and learning that guide a teacher's planning, teaching, and assessing. They provide the means to understand the need to establish a learning community within a classroom, and enable teachers to describe to administrators, parents, and colleagues why they implement the type of practice that they do.

The theoretical perspectives in this chapter include cognitive and developmental learning theory, social learning theory, critical theory, inquiry learning theory, and postmodern theory. The overall objective of the chapter is to ensure that teachers are aware of the broad range of perspectives that inform good teaching practice. Many educators have grown weary with theory (or theories), especially pertaining to education, and impatiently want to know what works. Many outside of education believe that they know about education merely because they have spent 12+ years in the system. Theirs is the only lens by which they judge education and its myriad complexities. Just as the journey of discovery about teaching and learning spans history (Dewey, 1933/1909, 1938, 1964; Friere, 2000; Kincheloe, Slattery, & Steinberg, 2000; Malaguzzi, 1994; Piaget, 1973; Vygotsky, 1978), you as the reader will continue to discern and construct information about the true nature of the complex acts involved in teaching and learning. Let the event begin.

Cognitive and Developmental Theories

Cognitive and developmental psychology provide theoretical lenses that focus on the dynamic relationship between learning and thinking. When observers confront the famous icon of Rodin's *The Thinker,* most wonder, what could the figure be contemplating? Maybe one questions the figure, "A penny for your thoughts?" Whatever the figure prompts in your thinking, it was Vygotsky (1962) who questioned the interrelationship between thought and language.

Jean Piaget and Barbel Inhelder (1973) described the ways in which humans construct knowledge, the premise from this point of view being that children learn much differently than adults. Piaget suggested that the developing child builds cognitive structures—mental "maps," schema, or networked concepts— for understanding and responding to physical experiences within the environment. He indicated that a child's cognitive structure increases in sophistication as the child develops, moving from a few innate reflexes such as crying and sucking to highly complex mental activities.

Piaget's theory identifies four developmental stages through which children progress:

- *Sensorimotor* stage (birth–2 years old): The child interacts with the physical environment, and in the process builds an understanding about reality and how it works. This is the stage where a child does not know that physical objects remain in existence even when out of sight (object permanence).

- *Preoperational* stage (ages 2–7): The child cannot conceptualize abstractly but learns through concrete, physical interactions with things in the environment. The ability to use symbols and representations were hallmarks of this stage.

- *Concrete* operational stage (ages 7–11): The child begins to create logical structures—concepts—that explain his or her physical experiences. The child also starts to engage in abstract problem solving at this stage. For example, arithmetic equations can be solved with numbers, not just with objects.

- Formal operations (beginning at ages 11–15): The child's cognitive structures begin to act like those of an adult and include conceptual reasoning. Hypothetical thinking was a feature of this stage.

Piaget suggested several principles for building cognitive structures to extend a child's learning. At each stage of development, children learn by using the mental maps they have constructed so far. Through repeated experience, children are able to fit new concepts into their mental maps and assimilate them into their cognitive structures. Children are also able to accommodate new or different experiences by altering their cognitive structure to accommodate the new conditions. In this way, children erect more and more adequate cognitive structures.

Piaget's theory has direct implications for educators, since they must plan a developmentally appropriate curriculum that enhances their students' logical and conceptual growth. Further, teachers must realize the critical role that experiences and interactions with the surrounding environment play in student learning, and plan their lessons accordingly. Piaget and Inhelder's theories suggest the need to base learning on what learners already know and to take into account the myriad factors—people, objects, language, and culture—that interact with the internal cognitive self-regulations that produce knowledge (Gallagher & Reid, 2002).

Jerome Bruner (1966) is often classified as a constructivist theorist, since he provides a general framework for instruction based upon the study of cognition. A major theme in Bruner's earlier theoretical framework is that learning is an active process in which learners construct new ideas or concepts based upon their current/past knowledge. The learner selects and transforms information, constructs hypotheses, and makes decisions, relying on a cognitive structure to do so. Cognitive structure (i.e., schema, mental models) provides meaning and organization to experiences and allows the individual to "go beyond the information given."

His work builds upon Piaget's theoretical efforts. Environmental and experimental factors play heavily on learning contexts and the learners' motives in Bruner's theoretical framework. The learners' interests and a readiness to learn are notable in this theory. In-depth learning rather than memorization, Bruner believes, is learning that is retained. He asserts that inquiry, problem solving, and discovery learning are features that cause permanent accommodation, which are changes in the cognitive structures.

These theoretical assumptions imply that teachers should try and encourage students to discover principles by themselves through the use of active dialogue (i.e., Socratic learning). The teacher's task is to translate information to be learned into a format appropriate to the learner's current state of understanding. Curriculum should be organized in a spiral manner so that the student continually builds upon what they have already learned.

In later years Bruner emphasized the central importance of culture. He suggested that culture shapes the mind and provides the toolkit by which we construct our worlds and the very conception of our selves and our powers. This orientation presupposes that human mental activity is neither individually oriented nor conducted unassisted, even when it goes on "inside the head."

Bruner's theory of instruction (1966) includes the following learner centered principles:

- Instruction is concerned with the experiences and contexts that student environments are planned for (readiness and ability to learn).
- Instruction is structured so that it can be easily grasped by the student (spiral organization).

- Instruction is designed to facilitate extrapolation and/or fill in the gaps (going beyond the information given).

Howard Gardner (2006) built upon Bruner's work in constructing a theory of multiple intelligences (MI) that is comprehensively integrated with classroom practice. In doing so Gardner redefined the word itself and the educational meaning of intelligence. The eight intelligences that Gardner described are biopsychological propensities through which human beings process information within familiar contexts. Gardner theorizes that it is in the intersection of thinking and problem solving within culturally relevant settings that individuals construct a uniquely personal perspective. The eight intelligences Gardner (1999) proposes include a nonexhaustive list comprised of:

- Bodily/kinesthetic

- Interpersonal

- Intrapersonal

- Linguistic

- Logical/mathematical

- Musical

- Naturalist

- Spatial

Elliot Eisner (1997) supports Gardner's form of thinking, maintaining that knowers come to know in a variety of ways, constructing knowledge as a result of experience. He states that acculturation enables learners to acquire the particular language, and accepted cultural expectations and norms of social groups of which they are part.

Caine and Caine (2006), as brain theorists, concur in a general way with the above theorists, examining brain functions through technological/medical concepts that increase our understanding of cognitive development. They suggest that learners have an innate biological potential and are prepared at birth to cognitively process and learn from experience, making myriad daily decisions in order to make sense of their environment. Teachers can capitalize on this capacity and potential, using processes of cognitive and developmental inquiry to make learning relevant, spark students' interests, and integrate a variety of content areas.

Caine and Caine (2006) suggest three effective strategies through which teachers can maximize student learning. First, scaffolding learning is important, helping learners progress from fundamental to more abstract, advanced thinking and understanding that increases the possibility of in-depth, high-interest learning. They also suggest that democratic environments in which teachers and students collaboratively establish rules and interactive learning strategies enable students to learn effectively and efficiently. Last, they assert that assessment must contain a variety of options that enable learners to have a voice in assessment procedures.

The cognitive and developmental theories presented above differ in detail and orientation to some degree, but all point to the need for teachers to understand the nature of human development, and the processes of acquiring new knowledge and skills. They indicate the importance of recognizing the stages of development through which learners necessarily travel as they acquire the ability to increase the complexity of their learning, and the need to carefully take account of the social environment within which each has learned to see and interact with the world. As we move through the book, therefore, the need for careful processes of inquiry and reflection that are a fundamental part of action research processes will become ever more evident.

SOCIAL LEARNING THEORY

A range of theories show that how children think—their cognitive development—is affected in fundamental ways by the social and cultural environment in which they are raised. Albert Bandura (1965) suggested that children learn through social imitation and observation of others' behavior. Since the 1980s his theoretical position has been congruous with the autonomous and reflective processes in cognitive change or accommodation suggested by Piaget (1973). Bandura's theory points to the interplay of personal, behavioral, and environmental influences and cognitive processes such as reflection, organizing information, decision making, and regulation of behavior (Bandura, 1986). He focuses on the importance of self-efficacy, imitation, and modeling—the ability to perceive others' actions and events and understand how individuals learn from what they see modeled.

Vygotsky (1978) asserted that culture is the prime determinant of an individual's cognitive development, and that the two dynamic processes associated with learning are language and social interaction. Children develop in the context of a culture, including the culture of a family environment, through which they acquire much of the content of their thinking—their knowledge. Culture, in other words, shows children both what to think and how to think.

Vygotsky suggested that cognitive development results from a dialectical process whereby a child learns through interaction with someone else, initially with family members, siblings, caregivers, and later with people like friends and teachers. Language is a primary form of interaction through which adults assist the child to develop the rich body of knowledge that exists in their culture. Since much of what a child learns comes from the child's home and community culture, Vygotsky's insight indicated that it is wrong to focus on a child in isolation. Such a focus does not reveal the processes by which children build knowledge and skills, or the base of existing knowledge from which the child can acquire new knowledge.

This perspective has many implications for teaching and learning. Learning activities should be designed to emphasize interaction between learners and associated learning tasks, starting from the knowledge and ways of thinking that come from their home culture. This relates to Vygotsky's conception of a zone of proximal development (ZPD). It is the place of potential where children are ready for adults, caregivers, teachers, or peers to facilitate learning. Learning commences in the "zone" known by the child, providing the point at which it is possible to introduce learning of a particular skill, concept, or generalization independently.

Vygotsky's perspective has been complemented by other theorists who explore the interaction between the individual (who is the knower), the environment, and the known—knowledge (DeVries & Kohlberg, 1987). Eisner (1987) maintains that the senses are an important part of the process of learning, providing multiple inputs that enable complex learning to occur. The complexity of the relationship between thought and language also has been the subject of intense debate. Kincheloe, Slattery, and Steinberg (2000) maintain that the relationship between thought and language involves a process of meaning making, in which learners "make sense" of new information by exploring connections with their existing knowledge.

INQUIRY LEARNING

Inquiry learning is based on a theoretical perspective initially presented by John Dewey. Like the cognitive and developmental theorists, he envisioned learners as curious beings at birth who move to higher stages of attention as they encounter the social world (Dewey, 1933/1909). Democracy, agency, and emancipation are hallmarks of Dewey's work in thinking and learning for school-aged children, and he notes that freedom is learned and achieved through multiple means of collaborative and relevant problem solving. In terms similar to those of Piaget, Dewey envisaged learners shifting from concrete operational positions to more formal or critical modes of thinking about problems or dilemmas.

Active learning is another term originally associated with Dewey. Cognitive connections are made through multisensory interaction that forms the basis for the experiential education that Dewey values so highly. Since the 1930s Dewey's ideas have challenged the traditional modes of education and provided a progressive and humanistic ideal that he considers to be in harmony with democratic social values. Dewey articulates dismay about the dominant voice of the teacher (1933/1909) and the silence of students. He finds it troubling that children's questioning and dialoguing are often discouraged. Dewey (1938) presented the notion of students learning together with teachers as ideal curricular practice, seeing reciprocity in learning as integral to schooling.

Questioning was another Deweyian tenet that pertained to both students and teachers, and thus he is known for his focus on student learning through inquiry. He views questioning as a means to push the boundaries of teachers' and students' reflective thinking. His questioning of traditional teaching practices often extends to the use of textbooks, posing the question of whether textbooks challenge or stifle the development of learners. Dewey envisions textbooks as supplements or resources only when students are in pursuit of solving a challenge of curiosity.

POSTMODERN PERSPECTIVES

Postmodern social theories emphasize the "locality" of influences affecting student and teacher learning. While cognitive theories provide broad insights into the nature of learning for all, postmodern theories emphasize the influences of the social environment or the context, and the need to take into account the "systems of meaning" that enable students from any particular locale, family, ethnic, or class setting to "make sense" of their environment and formulate appropriate ways of talking, acting, and feeling.

Fundamental to postmodernism are contextual aspects of all situations— philosophical, social, cultural, and historical issues that have as much impact on child learning as other considerations. From a postmodern perspective, teachers should become autonomous thinkers, able to function within diverse contexts and take into account the diverse influences on the local situation—cosmopolitanism, globalism, transnationalism, and so on (Aldridge & Goldman, 2007; Appiah, 2006; Elkind, 1995; Kincheloe, 2001; Nussbaum, 1997). Postmodern theorists analyze and question the often unvoiced assumptions that are part of any social context, and speak of the need to take notice of voices that have traditionally been excluded from decision making in the school. They suggest that the power of experts, political leaders, and highly educated professional elite impose their definitions of the situation. Their interpretations of situations often prevent "ordinary" people from having equitable influence on the services affecting their lives. Established social structures thus often exclude the voices of people in poverty, working and middle classes, and other marginalized racial and ethnic groups. Postmodernist theorists condemn the processes by which knowledge valued by power brokers usurps all others and disempowers marginalized peoples.

Postmodern theorists envision diversity and pluralism as essential to the educative arena. Educators who lean toward a postmodern perspective are committed to social and economic justice and seek to understand the reality of social contexts within which they work. In previous times situations have been defined by elite classes that have interpreted history in their own terms (Aldridge & Goldman, 2007; Elkind, 1995; Kincheloe, 2001). School texts, for instance, often described the Native American people first encountered by European explorers as "savages." Currently many Native American groups are called by tribal names that are incorrect and/or insulting (Loewen, 1999). In these cases, the first people on this land were conquered and had their land taken, suffered abuse at the hands of European Americans, and still are offended by historic misinterpretation and verbal pejoratives.

The postmodern perspective suggests the need for teachers to gain an understanding of the way others construct their lives according to the meanings and taken-for-granted behaviors and practices that are embedded in their everyday social world. Where programs and activities are based solely on interpretations and judgments of teachers, or where faulty or incorrect assumptions stemming from the teachers' own experiences and perspectives are used to formulate teaching and learning strategies, then student learning suffers. They fail to work effectively because they bear little relationship to the students' meanings, interpretations, and experiences.

The action research processes described in this book therefore provide the basis for processes of inquiry that are built into the everyday teaching and learning processes in any classroom. Through the systematic inquiry embedded in all learning routines, teachers and students together may embark on a journey of discovery that is educationally enlightening and enhances the learning potential of the students.

CRITICAL THEORY

Critical theory provides a systematic means to critique the prevalent technical theories of curriculum and instruction. Additionally, it offers an alternative approach to teaching and learning that enables educators to reflect on their practice (Carr & Kemmis, 1986). Critical theory helps us understand what happens when we fail to take into account the richness of cultural knowledge that "walks into the classroom" with our students.

Paulo Friere (1970) suggested that children's cultural capital—the knowledge children bring to school from their home and cultural environment—should be welcomed and utilized in school for teaching and knowledge building purposes. Teachers who practice critical pedagogy understand the perceptions and perspectives of their students, and the way they see the world (Kincheloe, Slattery, & Steinberg, 2000). This type of teacher would invite a mother in from the *barrio*, a Mexican American neighborhood, to make tortillas for a math lesson that integrates geometry into the lesson. In this way the knowledge of the culture of the community is celebrated and utilized in a relevant manner.

Peter McLaren (2006) analyzes challenging contemporary issues from a critical pedagogical perspective. Issues of class, ethnicity, power, gender, sexual orientation, and race are central aspects of critical theory, and his radically Marxist critical pedagogy is often difficult for teachers to accept. Those who have little experience of cultures other than their own frequently face disequilibrium with McLaren's perspective. It is a challenging one that confronts many of the assumptions of capitalistic life in the United States. Teachers and candidates may want to continue in comfort without examining uncomfortable issues. By confronting critical issues and rethinking assumptions that are part of their lifelong experience, teachers may take a path toward powerful and profound professional growth.

McLaren (2006) is keenly provocative, invoking readers to meet the challenges presented by the cultural and social assumptions that underlie their classroom practice. The questions woven into his text focus particularly on issues of social justice and equality and move teachers to provide solutions to the problems he presents. His questions precipitate consideration and discussion, and seem to be written for the purpose of extracting any one of them for in-depth, academic, or scholarly discussion. Possible frameworks are provided to problem-solve beyond discussion to conceive potential solutions.

Maxine Greene (1995) focuses on critical theory, counseling educators to be mindful of learners' lives and voices. Citizenship, she suggests, is first learned in the classroom, one of the first communities to which a child belongs. Questions related to issues of power, democracy, and justice enable learners and teachers to reveal the values and cultural meaning that are part of their learning experiences about citizenship. When teachers and learners actively solve problems together, they are able to envision how others live, believe, and perceive the world. Students are thus able to understand how culture is shaped through cyclic experiences of discovery, a process akin to the look, think, and act routine of action learning/research. Greene reminds us that critical theory has the potential to illuminate teachers' thinking and enhance their teaching practices.

This careful and thoughtful approach to inquiry and understanding is often termed *deconstruction*, encouraging teachers and learners to seek to understand "the entirety" of a text. By thoroughly inspecting the voids, the context, the historical considerations, the perspective of people with the least power, and the values of the educational theorists and historians, they are able to gain a better understanding of the ways that social and cultural considerations affect their classroom lives.

Transformative learning theory, stemming from critical theory, provides yet another perspective that influences our understanding of pedagogy. Through critical reflection upon the contexts and social, political, economic, and educational issues, action is undertaken to identify a problem, ponder assumptions about the situation, examine alternatives, elicit ideas from all involved in the situation, and then collaborate to achieve a mutual goal. This perspective points to the need to develop empathetic understandings and provide support to all participants in the setting (Mezirow, 1991).

The vignette about Ms. McKinley's sixth graders that begins this chapter provides an example of transformative learning theory in action. All participants were changed by the way their interaction became so meaningful within the context of their environment. They discovered that the assumptions they had about people of different ages did not stand up to scrutiny. Sixth-grade students, reflecting on their experience, found they needed to change long-held beliefs about the elders as they created Web sites and explored histories and music from another era. It was likewise evident in the final gathering that the entire process had transformed the way elders perceived the students.

CONCLUSION

These varying theoretical perspectives highlight the fact that teachers cannot assume that their "commonsense" view of the world, or the knowledge acquired in professional preparation, will "make sense" in the lives of the students they teach. The move to incorporate action research into the teaching/learning processes of a classroom, therefore, signals the need for teachers to approach the act of teaching as a process of inquiry and discovery. In doing so they will, over time, accumulate a body of knowledge and understanding that will enhance their professional lives and provide great satisfaction for their students. The chapters that follow, therefore, supply the means to simply and efficiently incorporate action research—an act of inquiry—into the regular routines of teaching and learning in a classroom.

None of the theoretical perspectives presented above is right or wrong in any definitive sense, but each provides a lens that highlights particular aspects of any classroom situation or process of learning. Think of these varied theories as a vast buffet from which you may choose according to the needs of the children in your classroom. The theories presented provide useful conceptual tools that may assist teachers to deal most effectively with the complex situations and sometimes apparently overwhelming dilemmas they face in their classrooms. Hopefully, what you glean from theories provides the basis for sound practice that is informed by the particular concepts and perspectives presented. They assist you to allow students to continue growing and learning, thus perpetuating a form of collaborative cognitive growth that enhances the classroom life of you and your students. This is the essence of action learning/research: look, think, and act.

LEARNING RESOURCES

Reflection

Look: In the Look phase of Ms. McKinley's social studies lesson (see beginning of the chapter), which of the INTASC standards (p. 29) and theories do you think she examined prior to determining this particular set of lessons for the project?

Think: In the Think phases listed in the vignette, which standards did Ms. McKinley enact? What about the students and how did they assist her to implement the theoretical stances of some of the theorists in the chapter? In what specific ways did the students' work reflect the theories?

Act: Again, in the vignette, which particular area of study and which theorists do you think most reflect what students accomplished with Ms. McKinley's assistance? What are some other ways in which the students could have elaborated on the project to encompass other theories and/or standards?

Web Sites

Jean Piaget:

http://webspace.ship.edu/cgboer/piaget.html

This is just one of a plethora of Web sites where you can research the myriad accomplishments and theories of the epistemologist, Jean Piaget.

www.unige.ch/piaget/biographies/biobiGB.html

This is an official Piagetian Web site. Be sure to have it translated as it is in French.

Lev Vygotsky:

http://starfsfolk.khi.is/solrunb/vygotsky.htm

This site will provide an overall historical view of Vygotsky and links to his contemporaries.

Jerome S. Bruner:

www.infed.org/thinkers/bruner.htm

This educational icon's life is thoroughly outlined. His work in a humanistic bent on cognitive and developmental theories is clarified.

Albert Bandura:

http://www.muskingum.edu/~psych/psycweb/history/bandura.htm

Bandura has come full circle from a behaviorist approach to social learning to a humanistic, developmental approach.

Paulo Freire:

www.paulofreireinstitute.org/

The institute's Web site offers visitors an abundance of links to learn about the paramount social justice teacher, prolific writer, and speaker. His life's work continues through the institute at UCLA.

Peter McLaren:

www.gseis.ucla.edu/faculty/pages/mclaren/

Radical seeker of justice, Peter McLaren is the "real thing." Peruse his Web site to see how a classroom teacher transformed into a person who lives his ideals as a democratic citizen for social justice.

Maxine Greene:

www.newfoundations.com/GALLERY/Greene.html

Maxine Greene is a renaissance woman. She was one of the first female presidents of American Educational Research Association, an inexhaustible writer, and a proponent of pluralism. Her vision is that aesthetic education programs can bring democracy to every child in school, especially where the arts are abandoned for scripted programs.

Additional Reading

Bruner, J. S. (1964). The course of cognitive growth. *American Psychologist, 79*, 1–15.

Bruner, J. S. (1971). *The relevance of education.* New York: Norton.

Caine, R. N., & Caine, G. (2006). The way we learn. *Educational Leadership, 64*(1), 50–54.

Carr, W., & Kemmis, S. (1986). *Becoming critical: Education, knowledge and action research.* London: Falmer.

DeVries, R., & Kohlberg, L. (1987). *Constructivist early education: Overview and comparison with other programs.* Washington, DC: NAEYC.

Dewey, J. (1933). *How we think: A restatement of the relation of reflective thinking to the educative process* (Rev. ed.). Boston: Heath. (Original work published 1909)

Dewey, J. (1938). *Experience and education.* New York: Macmillan Publishing Company.

Dewey, J. (1964). The relation of theory to practice in education. In R. D. Archambault (Ed.), *John Dewey on education* (pp. 313–338). Chicago: University of Chicago Press.

Dick, B. (1997). *Action learning and action research.* Retrieved February 8, 2007, from www.scu.edu.au/schools/gcm/ar/arp/actlearn.html

Eisner, E. W. (1987). *Cognition and curriculum.* New York: Longman.

Eisner, E. W. (1997). *Enlightened eye: Qualitative inquiry and the enhancement of educational practice* (2nd ed.). New York: Merrill Publishing Company.

Elkind, D. (1995). School and family in the postmodern world. *Phi Delta Kappan, 76*, 8–14.

Friere, P. (2000). *Pedagogy of freedom: Ethics, democracy, and civic courage.* Lanham, MD: Rowman & Littlefield Publishers.

Gallagher, J. M., & Reid, D. K. (2002). *The learning theory of Piaget and Inhelder.* New York: Authors Choice Press.

Gardner, H. (1993). *Frames of mind: The theory of multiple intelligences* (2nd ed.). New York: Basic Books.

Gardner, H. (1999). *Intelligence reframed: Multiple intelligences for the 21st century.* New York: Basic Books.

Gardner, H. (2006). *The development and education of the mind: The selected works of Howard Gardner.* New York: Routledge.

Kincheloe, J. L. (2001). *Getting beyond the facts: Teaching social studies/social sciences in the twenty-first century* (2nd ed.). New York: Peter Lang Publishing.

Kincheloe, J. L., Slattery, P., & Steinberg, S. R. (2000). *Contextualizing teaching: Introduction to education and educational foundations.* NY: Addison, Wesley & Longman.

Loewen, J. W. (1999). *Lies across America: What our historic sites get wrong.* New York: The New Press.

Malaguzzi, L. (1994). Listening to children. *Young Children, 49*(5), 55.

McLaren, P. (2006). *Life in schools: An introduction to critical pedagogy in the foundations of education* (5th ed.). New York: Allyn & Bacon.

Mezirow, J. (1991). *Transformative dimensions of adult learning and fostering critical reflection in adulthood: A guide to transformative and emancipatory learning.* Hoboken, NJ: Jossey-Bass.

Overton, W. F. (1998). Developmental psychology: Philosophy, concepts, and methodology. In R. M. Lerner (Ed.), *Theoretical models of human development. Vol. 1: Handbook of child psychology* (5th ed., pp. 107–188). New York: Wiley.

Overton, W. F., & Palermo, D. S. (Eds.). (1994). *The nature and ontogenesis of meaning.* Hillsdale, NJ: Lawrence Erlbaum.

Piaget, J. (1973). *To understand is to invent: The future of education.* New York: Grossman.

Schon, D. (1983). *The reflective practitioner.* New York: Basic Books.

Stringer, E. T. (1996). *Action research: A handbook for practitioners.* Thousand Oaks, CA: Sage.

Vygotsky, L. (1978). *Mind and society.* Cambridge, MA: Harvard University Press.

Teaching Standards: Interstate New Teacher Assessment Support Consortium (INTASC) Principles

TEACHER PRINCIPLES

Principle 1   The teacher understands the central concepts, tools of inquiry, and structure of the disciplines he or she teaches and can create learning experiences that make these aspects of subject matter meaningful for students.

Principle 2   The teacher understands how children learn and develop, and can provide learning opportunities that support their intellectual, social, and personal development.

Principle 3   The teacher understands how students differ in their approaches to learning and creates instructional opportunities that are adapted to diverse learners.

Principle 4   The teacher understands and uses a variety of instructional strategies to encourage students' development of critical thinking, problem-solving, and performance skills.

Principle 5   The teacher uses an understanding of individual and group motivation and behavior to create a learning environment that encourages positive social interaction, active engagement in learning, and self-motivation.

Principle 6   The teacher uses knowledge of effective verbal, nonverbal, and media communication techniques to foster active inquiry, collaboration, and supportive interaction in the classroom.

Principle 7   The teacher plans instruction based upon knowledge of subject matter, students, the community, and curriculum goals.

Principle 8   The teacher understands and uses formal and informal assessment strategies to evaluate and ensure the continuous intellectual, social, and physical development of the learner.

Principle 9   The teacher is a reflective practitioner who continually evaluates the effects of his or her choices and actions on others (students, parents, and other professionals in the learning community) and who actively seeks out opportunities to grow professionally.

Principle 10   The teacher fosters relationships with school colleagues, parents, and agencies in the larger community to support students' learning and well-being.

CHAPTER **3**

Lesson Planning

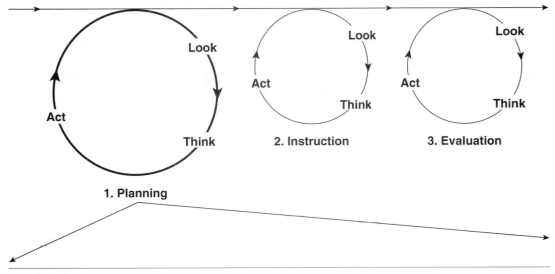

Planning Phase

This chapter focuses on lesson planning. It describes how to use an action research Look–Think–Act routine to prepare a lesson or unit of study:

Review instructional elements—student prior knowledge, student characteristics, community context, state standards (Look)

Select and organize appropriate instructional components (Think)

Construct a lesson plan (Act)

The chapter then describes how to apply this process within a direct instruction approach to teaching:

- *Preparation:* Teachers describe lesson objectives and review existing student knowledge (Look), arouse student interest through reflection (Think), and report and clarify lesson activities (Act).

31

- *Presentation:* Teacher input (Look), checking for understanding (Think), student perform/practice (Act)

- *Practice:* Review/repeat (Look), reflect/check (Think), perform (Act)

The chapter then applies the process to the three phases of an inquiry learning lesson:

- *Exploration:* Prior knowledge (Look), ideas and concepts (Think), record and organize (Act)

- *Development:* Acquire information (Look), reason (Think), document (Act)

- *Expansion:* Review (Look), reflect (Think), apply and assess (Act)

NAVIGATING COMPLEXITY: LEARNING TO PLAN LESSONS

I clearly remember the first lesson I presented on teaching practice. I had carefully prepared the steps of the lesson and organized necessary materials, so that by the end of the lesson I felt that I had successfully accomplished my first teaching task. Later, my supervising teacher provided me feedback that was, I must admit, very deflating. She kindly pointed out to me many of the things I had failed to do, the deficiencies in my explanations and modeling, my failure to monitor student performance, and so on.

It was at this point that I realized there was much more to teaching than standing in front of the class, providing them information and having them recall and record what they had heard and read. For the first time it became clear to me that the long lists of requirements and processes provided in my college classes actually had a purpose and a meaning in the classroom. The task, at that stage, became quite daunting. How, I thought, can I possibly remember to do all that? "How," I thought, "can I possibly deal with the mountain of detail that's involved? I thought this would be relatively straightforward, but it's HUGE."

In time I acquired the capacity to encompass the broad range of issues that need to be taken into account in planning lessons, presenting lessons, and assessing student performance. I now feel comfortable and competent as a classroom teacher, but know that I have in my head a number of frameworks, heuristics, and rubrics that provide a "pattern" for me to follow as I plan my lessons and work with my students.

The frameworks that follow have, for a number of years now, guided my thinking wherever and whenever I am called to act in a teaching capacity. They provide a simple set of routines and recipes that enable me to negotiate the complex array of tasks and requirements that are part of any classroom setting. They do not describe the "reality" of what happens, or should happen in teaching, but act as a compass or a set of guidelines that keep me on track as I navigate the complex waters of classroom life. The ongoing "research" assists me to deal with the wide variety of issues that confront me as I work with my students. Research, I have said elsewhere (Stringer, 2007), is the process of seeking understanding in the company of friends.

This, likewise, signals another aspect of my teaching—that it is not a set of mechanical routines, but processes of communication and interaction that, when well enacted, provide me with the rich rewards that come from students who know they have accomplished something worthwhile.

—E.S.

As the previous chapter has made clear, and the above account illustrates, effective teaching needs to take into account a wide range of factors, provide a variety of activities to accomplish diverse outcomes required of any educational program, and make use of learning resources and materials that are a necessary part of classroom learning. Teachers have to consider:

- Varying levels of students' knowledge, ability, and experience
- Ways of focusing students' attention
- Ways of relating prior knowledge to new learning
- The availability of necessary teaching/learning materials
- State standards in each content area
- Information available from standardized tests and other information sources (Sunal & Haas, 2008)

In the sections that follow, we show how action research processes can enhance lesson planning by providing the cues that enable teachers to take account of these multiple issues. We first present a general model that provides details of procedures for using action research as the basis for lesson planning. We then show how this model is applied to two approaches to teaching—direct instruction and inquiry learning.

PREPARING A UNIT OF STUDY (LESSON)

The simple Look–Think–Act action research routine assists teachers to clarify the lesson planning process presented in the previous chapter, enabling them to formulate well-organized, interesting, and effective lessons that engage children's attention and enable them to achieve high standards of learning. Teachers start by determining what is to be learned by the children—the topic of the unit of study (Focus). They then review instructional elements (LOOK—information gathering), select and organize lesson components—content, learning strategies, and activities (THINK—analysis), and construct a lesson plan (ACT—lesson plan). Each of these activities focuses on the type of issues described in Figure 3.1.

LOOK: FOCUSING AND REVIEWING

The first stage in lesson planning is to select a unit of study that will provide the basis for productive and interesting learning experiences for students. The unit of study should be relevant to the students' age and stage of development, and to their family and community experiences. It should also incorporate learning activities that enable

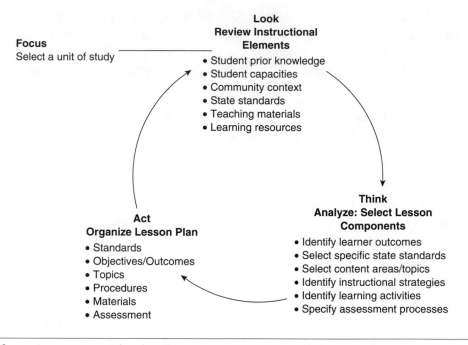

Figure 3.1 Lesson Planning Steps

students to accomplish the broad range of standards mandated by the state, and should specify assessment activities through which students will demonstrate the level of competencies they have acquired.

Student Knowledge, Experiences, Interests, and Capacities

Teachers reflect on questions that orient the planning process to the perspectives, interests, and experiences of students. They start with the world of the child and use that to lead them to new, interesting, and challenging learning experiences. They ask:

- Who are my students?

- What do they know?

- What are they capable of doing?

- What are their interests?

- What issues concern them?

- Who are their families?

- What is the nature of the community?

- What do they experience in their daily lives?

- What community strengths and resources can enhance student learning?

Identifying a Unit of Study

Teachers select a unit of study that is relevant to student learning needs and state standards. They ask:

- What do my students know? What are the gaps in their *knowledge?*
- What *skills* do they need to develop?
- What standards are relevant to these needs?
- What topics or content areas will provide a focus for teaching/learning?

Identifying Instructional Elements

Teachers then review state standards. They identify instructional strategies and learning activities that are relevant to those standards. They reflect on the teaching materials and learning resources available in the classroom, school, family, and community. They ask:

- How can students accomplish the state standards?
- What learning experiences can I provide for my students?
- What procedures will I use to introduce topics and monitor progress?
- What materials and resources do we need?
- What do I have in the classroom?
- What is in the school? Student homes? The community?
- How can parents contribute, assist?

Responses to these questions provide a teacher with a large body of information that then needs to be carefully distilled, organized, and used as the basis for a lesson plan. The next phase therefore involves a careful process of selection and organization.

THINK: SELECTING AND ORGANIZING

Having identified the unit of study and reviewed instructional elements, teachers carefully identify the specific content areas, teaching strategies, and learning activities that will enable students to accomplish the selected standards. They first identify a set of objectives or outcomes, and then select the standards to which those outcomes are relevant. They also identify ways that students will demonstrate they have successfully accomplished the objectives.

Objectives/Outcomes

Teachers identify a set of objectives or outcomes that frame the unit of study. They ask:

- What objectives or outcomes will be the focus of the lesson?
- What should my students know or be able to do when they have completed this unit of study?

State Standards

Teachers identify the key standards relevant to the objectives. They ask:

- What standards will the students have achieved when they complete this unit of study?

Content Areas or Subtopics

Teachers select areas of study or subtopics that will be included in the unit of study. They ask:

- What topics shall I include in the unit of study that are relevant to my students' interests, experiences, and learning needs?

Instructional Strategies

Teachers devise steps they will take to initiate and facilitate student learning. They ask:

- What shall I do to initiate the lesson?
- What shall I do to lead them through the steps or stages of the learning cycle?
- What strategies shall I implement for this particular group of learners?

Learning Activities

Teachers devise activities that will enable students to identify and build on existing knowledge, or to learn new skills. They ask:

- What activities can students engage in to extend their knowledge, understanding, or skills in relation to the topic or area of study?
- What activities will assist them to attain proficiency in the standards?

Assessment[1]

Teachers select ways of assessing student performance in relation to the outcomes and standards selected for the unit of study. They ask:

- How can students demonstrate they have successfully achieved each of the outcomes?

- Have these outcomes enabled students to accomplish state standards?

- How can I assess the quality of their performance? What criteria shall I use? Do I need an assessment rubric?

ACT: WRITING A LESSON PLAN

Teachers organize the selected elements into a coherent lesson plan that sets out the sequence of activities required to accomplish student learning objectives/outcomes. The above information is assembled into a lesson plan that incorporates:

- *Objectives/Outcomes:* The central focus of the lesson—what students will know and be able to do by the end of the lesson

- *Standards*: State requirements associated with outcomes

- *Procedures*: A sequence of learning activities

- *Assessment*: Tasks that enable each student to demonstrate a level of performance on each of the outcomes

- *Materials*: Materials and equipment required during the lesson

Teachers commonly construct lesson plans within a grid or table (see Figure 3.2) that enables them to check the progress of the lesson as students move through the sets of learning activities and assessment tasks.

PLANNING DIRECT INSTRUCTION LESSONS

Direct instruction is a widely used model of instruction. It is particularly effective where students need to learn specific skills or to be introduced to a new topic or area of study. Simplistic formulations of direct instruction focus on teacher presentation and student recall, but as proponents of direct instruction acknowledge, effective

Grade Level:	
Subject:	
Unit Title/Lesson Title:	
Time/Duration:	
Content Area Standards:	
Special Needs and ELL and Bilingual Modifications and Accommodations:	

Materials			
Objectives/ Outcomes & Standards	**Teacher Procedures**	**Student Procedures**	**Assessment**

Figure 3.2   Lesson Planning Grid

learning requires a much more complex process of inquiry and exploration. The various models of direct instruction (Huitt, 2003; Hunter, 1990/1991; Rosenshine, 1995; Slavin, 2006) include specific elements that outline the lesson procedure. The planning of the lesson includes the identification of the objectives/outcomes—what students should know and/or be able to do as a result of the lesson—and their alignment with performance standards. The presentation of the lesson begins with the teacher's utilization of a method for connecting what students have already learned to what is to be learned, thus, focusing students' attention. Next, the teacher explains and models the concept or skill, following with a check for understanding of the concept or skill. Then, students engage in guided practice with the teacher monitoring student progress. The important stage of closure that follows guided practice provides students with a means to organize, summarize, and reflect on what they have been taught and what they have learned. The final aspect, independent practice, is the student application of the new information as a demonstration of understanding of the new information, concept, or skill.

Teachers can enhance a direct instruction lesson by systematically incorporating action research processes of inquiry into each phase of a lesson. The intent is to provide students with rich, rewarding learning experiences that provoke their interest and provide them with knowledge and skills that can be applied to their lives in meaningful ways. Teachers start by asking questions that enable students to link the subject matter to their existing knowledge and community/family experience. The following sections therefore describe how the Look–Think–Act action learning routine can be incorporated into direct instruction lessons.

ELEMENTS OF DIRECT INSTRUCTION

Elements of direct instruction (Hunter, 1990/1991) include:

- Objectives: What the student will be able to do or know as a result of instruction
- Standards: The standards of performance to be expected of the student
- Anticipatory set: How to focus student attention on the lesson
- Teaching/presentation: Teacher activities that include
  - Input, in which the teacher provides information
  - Modeling, in which the teacher demonstrates what is expected of the student
- Checking for student understanding or skill competence
- Guided practice/monitoring
- Closure
- Independent practice

PHASES OF INSTRUCTION

These elements can be organized to reflect three phases of an instructional process—Preparation, Presentation, and Practice. The Look–Think–Act framework is applied to each phase to clearly identify different types of activity-acquiring information, reflecting or analyzing, and engaging in activities (see Figure 3.3).

Preparation

- Anticipatory set: Describe objectives and review prior knowledge
- Focus student attention: Review class activities and expected outcomes
- Report, record, and clarify issues

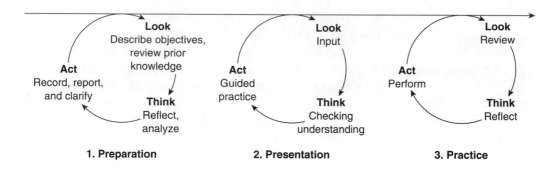

Figure 3.3   Phases of Direct Instruction

Presentation

- Input/modeling
- Checking for understanding
- Guided practice

Practice

- Review/repeat
- Reflect
- Perform

Phase 1: Preparation—Anticipatory Set

In this phase teachers prepare their students for the lesson to come. They present the focus or topic of the lesson and the objectives and outcomes to be achieved. Teachers also inform students of the activities in which they will be engaged. The teacher ascertains students' existing knowledge and skill levels in the area to be covered (see Figure 3.4).

Review objectives and prior knowledge (Look). Students are presented with a clear idea of the *objectives* of the lesson and the *outcomes* they need to achieve in performance or behavioral terms. Teachers assist students to review their prior knowledge and/or demonstrate existing skill levels.

Review, reflect, and focus (Think). Teachers arouse students' interest, referring to experiences and interests they have had that might be linked to the subject matter. Teachers formulate questions or pose problems that can be presented to students to

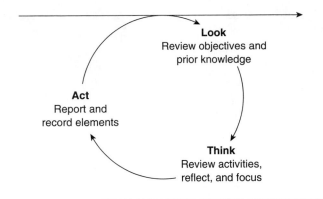

Figure 3.4   Preparation Cycle

stimulate their interest and foster their exploration of the topic. They may also prepare activities that have this function—puzzles, field trips, guest speakers, and so on—to introduce students to the topic in an interesting way.

Sharing and recording (Act). Students reflect on and analyze their existing knowledge, identifying, sharing, and recording some of the key elements of the topic.

Phase 2: Presentation—Input/Modeling, Checking, Practicing

Teachers engage students in a wide range of activities to enable them to acquire the designated information and skills (see Chapter 5)—teacher presentations, guest speakers, videos, documentaries, books, community events, and so on. Students may also engage in processes of exploration and discovery that enhance their ability to learn independently, and to follow paths that are particularly interesting.

In this phase teachers engage in *modeling* activities that demonstrate what is to be learned by the students. They also provide clear *directions* to ensure students know precisely *what* they will do, and *how* they will do it. This is the "Look" step of Presentation (see Figure 3.5).

Teachers also plan how they will *check for understanding,* evaluating and analyzing students' performance by asking appropriate questions, observing student activities, or viewing the products of student work. Again, teachers will prepare questions that include all levels of objectives—knowledge, comprehension, application, analysis, synthesis, and evaluation. These constitute the "Think" step of Presentation (see Figure 3.5).

Lessons will also include activities that enable students to *apply* or *use* the knowledge/skills they have acquired. These will be carried out under the direct supervision

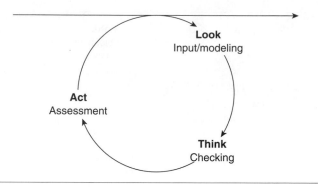

Figure 3.5   Presentation Cycle

of the teacher who will provide instructions, breaking each activity into parts or a sequence of steps that enable students to systematically master the knowledge or skills to be learned. Teachers should plan for repeated student trials so they can provide remediation where required—the "Act" step of Presentation (see Figure 3.5).

Input/modeling (Look). Teachers prepare students for the lesson, and then provide information through lecture presentations, books, videos, pictures, and so on. They model the way that information may be used or applied. They explain the critical aspects or key elements of the information.

Checking for understanding (Think). Through questioning, observation, and assessment, teachers check that students have understood or can adequately perform what has been taught.

Assessment of student performance (Act). As students enact learning and assessment activities, teachers supervise their work, providing feedback on students' levels of mastery and individual remediation where needed.

Phase 3: PRACTICE—Review, Reflect, Repeat

In this phase, students reinforce their learning by engaging in independent practice of what they have learned. Teachers prepare projects or activities that enable students to practice or use the content or skills they have learned. Students will reinforce and extend what they know, and increase their skill levels by utilizing their new knowledge. Teachers may provide projects or tasks that students do independently, for example, as homework, or incorporated into subsequent lessons. As they engage these activities, students will review what they have learned (Look), reflect on previous performances or products (Think), and plan and practice what they need to do to improve their performance (Act) (see Figure 3.6).

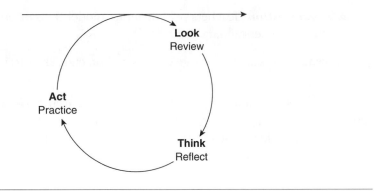

Figure 3.6   Practice Cycle

Review (Look). Students review what they have learned.

Reflect (Think). Students reflect on previous performances, noting any gaps or inadequacies. They thus evaluate previous performances and plan remediation.

Repeat (Act). Students demonstrate they have attained desired levels of performance through cycles of repetition and reflection.

CASE EXAMPLE 3.1: A PUBLIC SPEAKING LESSON (I)

This example presents the first of a sequence of two direct instruction lessons[2] that used action research procedures as a planning scaffold (see Figure 3.3). The teacher:

- *Reviewed instructional elements*—student prior knowledge, student capacities, state standards, community context, teaching materials, and learning resources (LOOK)

- Selected *lesson components* from the large number of possible standards, outcomes, content, instructional strategies, learning activities, and assessment procedures (THINK)

- Organized a *lesson plan* using a framework that includes standards, outcomes, teacher instructional activities, student learning activities, and assessment procedures (ACT)

The resulting lesson plan illustrates the outcomes of these procedures for a direct instruction lesson. It is presented as three phases of instruction:

1. **Preparation**: Teachers arouse student interest, review their existing knowledge and skills, and present an outline of activities.

2. **_Presentation_**: Teachers provide input, model skills or processes, and check student understanding.

3. **_Practice_**: Students engage in trials and practice skills to be learned.

Each phase includes cycles of the action research Look–Think–Act routine. Although the teaching/learning processes do not always neatly fit the Look–Think–Act steps, they provide the means to distinguish between activities associated with the different levels and types of educational objective:

- _Look:_ Acquiring knowledge

- _Think:_ Comprehension and analysis

- _Act:_ Using, applying, synthesizing, or evaluating

Subject: Language Arts

Grade: 7

Unit: Public Speaking

Topic: Persuasive Speech

Duration: Two 90 minute class periods: 1st phase (2nd phase in Chapter 5)

New Jersey State Standards Language Arts–Literacy

3.2 _Writing:_ D. Writing Forms, Audiences, and Purposes

3.3 _Speaking:_ A. Discussion. B. Questioning and Contributing. C. Word Choice. D. Oral Presentation

Materials: Papers, pencils, pens, direction sheet (guidelines for delivering a persuasive speech), pocket dictionary, topics for a persuasive speech

Accommodations/Modifications: One-on-one instruction if necessary, peer tutors, provide step-by-step instructions, have appropriate reading materials, check on progress regularly, have an aide and assistive technology if possible, work with a special educator to modify instruction

Bilingual English Language Learner Strategies: Peer tutors; labels in student(s)' language; word walls in native tongue and English; adapted texts; instructions and directions in representative/native language if possible; utilization of visuals such as pictorial schematics, graphic organizers, charts to illustrate concepts, directions, and so on

PHASE 1: PREPARATION—Anticipatory Set

Objectives/outcomes	Teacher instruction	Student learning	Assessment
Students will: Identify the elements of persuasive speech.	**Act** Teacher poses the following questions to students: How do your friends try to convince you about something or persuade you to side with them? Give us an example. What makes their argument effective? Give us an example of a speech you heard recently. How did the speaker convince you to consider his/her point of view? What made his/her speech persuasive?	**Look** Students listen to teacher. **Think** They reflect on their experience and formulate responses to teacher's questions.	
	Look Teacher listens to student responses.	**Act** Students offer examples of what they think is a speech (sermon, principal address to student body, etc.). They use their examples to discuss teacher questions.	**Look/Think** Teacher will note extent of student understanding of elements of persuasive speech.
	Think Teacher identifies key elements of a speech that students offer as example. **Act** Teacher writes speech elements on chalkboard. Teacher informs students they will be learning about persuasive speaking. She tells them that they will write a persuasive speech, practice it, and deliver it in class.	 Students copy notes from the chalkboard into their notebooks.	**Act** Teacher will record key elements of students' existing knowledge.

PHASE 2: PRESENTATION—Input/Modeling, Checking, Practicing

Objectives/outcomes	Teacher instruction	Student learning	Assessment
Students will: Recognize the elements of credibility in a persuasive speech.	**INPUT/MODELING** **Act** Teacher lists on chalkboard additional elements of persuasive speech and adds them to those identified by students listed on the chalkboard. Teacher presents a video demonstrating two examples of persuasive speaking. Teacher stops video at intervals to identify key elements of persuasive speaking and discuss the credibility of the arguments.	**LISTENING/ OBSERVING** **Look** Students add additional elements and discussion comments to their notes. **Think** Students refer to their notes and identify key elements in the videotaped speeches. Students discuss the points being made in each argument that are believable and those points that are weak.	
	CHECKING FOR UNDERSTANDING **Act** Teacher provides students an example of a persuasive speech and places transparency of speech on overhead projector. Teacher reads speech out loud and asks students to identify key elements. **Look/Think** Teacher asks students questions about elements to determine: • Basic knowledge • Critical thinking	**CHECKING FOR UNDERSTANDING** **Act** Students identify key elements and label them on their speech handout.	**Act** Teacher assesses levels of understanding of elements for each student.
Students will: Demonstrate understanding by preparing a persuasive speech.	**GUIDED PRACTICE** **Act** Teacher prepares students to write their own speeches. She asks students to identify topics about which they feel strongly and writes them on the chalkboard.	**GUIDED PRACTICE** **Look/Think** Each student selects a topic from the chalkboard list and identifies a position	

Objectives/outcomes	Teacher instruction	Student learning	Assessment
		(for or against) and an audience.	
	Teacher suggests that students use a web prewriting technique to organize thoughts and develop speech. Teacher models with an example.	**Act** Each student utilizes a web prewriting activity to organize his/her thinking and to develop chosen topic, placing topic in center of page and creating a "web" of related points.	**Act** Teacher records contents of student web that represent student understanding at this point in the development of speech.
	As students work, teacher circulates, making comments about elements and offering advice.		**Act** Teacher provides verbal feedback as formative assessment.

PHASE 3: PRACTICE (Independent Practice): Review, Reflect, Construct/Perform

Objectives/outcomes	Teacher instruction	Student learning	Assessment
	REVIEW **Look** The teacher asks students questions to review the day's lessons. The teacher presents students with a scoring guide with indicators to assess: • Understanding of elements of persuasive speech included in their presentation • Effectiveness of their presentation	**REVIEW** **Look** Students review, clarify, and summarize elements of persuasive speech by: • Responding to teacher questions • Checking chalkboard notes • Checking their own notes At home, students will review their notes and the "web" graphic organizers containing elements of persuasive speech on the topic they have selected.	

(Continued)

PHASE 3 (Continued)

Objectives/outcomes	Teacher instruction	Student learning	Assessment
		REFLECT **Think** Each student will add to, modify, and further develop the ideas and concepts in their "web" organizer. **CONSTRUCT** **Act** Using these ideas and concepts, they will write a draft of a persuasive speech on their selected topic.	Use the scoring guide to self-assess the draft they have written.

PLANNING INQUIRY LEARNING LESSONS

Inquiry learning is an approach to classroom instruction that uses investigation and inquiry as the major approach to student learning. Unlike direct instruction that focuses on teacher-generated knowledge, inquiry learning commences with the teacher assisting students to explore their existing knowledge, and uses that as the basis for further learning. The teacher does not tell the students what they will learn, but assists them to extend their knowledge in ways that are meaningful to them. By starting with what the child knows, teachers provide a sound cognitive base for an effective learning process. They assist their students to clarify and extend their existing knowledge, incorporating new elements logically and meaningfully into rich and varied curriculum content that enables children to accomplish a broad range of learning objectives.

An inquiry learning cycle assists students to identify their existing knowledge of a topic or issue, and develop new knowledge from that foundation (Sunal & Haas, 2008). This type of lesson plan allows teachers and students to include activities and strategies that focus on a developmental process of learning rather than being constrained by a fixed schedule. Teachers use action research to plan a program of flexible, student-centered learning activities that begin with students' current knowledge and interests, and incorporate required outcomes into each phase of the learning cycle.

In this book inquiry learning is framed by learning cycles that emerge in three phases (see Figure 3.7):

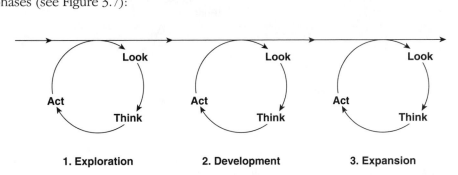

Figure 3.7   Phases of an Inquiry Learning Cycle

1. **Exploration**, in which students explore and reveal their *prior knowledge* of a topic

2. **Development**, where students use multisensory learning strategies to acquire *new concepts and skills*

3. **Expansion**, where students *apply* that knowledge in new and meaningful ways, and assess their learning

Throughout this process, the teacher acts as a guide and facilitator, providing generative questions, comments, and suggestions that assist students to extend, clarify, and enhance their learning.

In each phase, the Look–Think–Act routine of *action learning* (see Figure 5.2)[3] provides the basis for ongoing inquiry, ensuring that each component of a lesson is thoroughly grounded in a process of observation, reflection, and action.

Phase 1: EXPLORATION—Revealing Prior Knowledge

Phase 1 focuses students on the topic of what is to be studied. The first step engages learners in active experiences that focus their inquiry and exploration. In this phase, as suggested by Sunal and Hass (2008), students reveal their prior knowledge, self-correct misconceptions, and develop more accurate conceptions about the topic—the "Look" phase of learning (see Figure 3.8). Teachers use generative questions to assist students to identify what they know about the topic or issue (prior knowledge), and to stimulate their thinking. They also provide students with stimulus materials to engage in exploratory tasks that stimulate their thinking—the "Think" phase of learning (see Figure 3.8). In small groups students organize and record information—the "Act" phase of learning (see Figure 3.8).

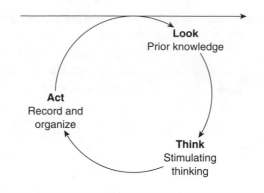

Figure 3.8   Exploration Phase of Inquiry Learning

Identify prior knowledge (Look). Students identify what they know about the topic.

Generate ideas and concepts (Think). The teacher provides key questions and learning materials (photos, manipulatives, etc.) to stimulate student thinking and assist them to investigate the topic further.

Talk, record, and organize (Act). Students discuss the topic, record the emerging information, and plan how they will organize it.

Phase 2: DEVELOPMENT—Processing, Reasoning, and Documenting

Students explore the topic further, gathering information from a variety of sources—the "Look" phase of the development cycle (see Figure 3.9). Teachers assist students to extend their learning by processing the data gathered in the "Exploration" phase and providing more input, information. Development builds on the exploratory introduction. In this phase of the lesson plan, students report back on their findings from the exploration phase. For younger students, teachers document on chart paper, chalk, or whiteboards what students have found and discovered from exploration. This action serves not only to document learning but also visually fills voids in some students' background knowledge. Students are expected to explain how their findings are related to their responses to the exploratory introduction activity.

This is the phase where the "real work" begins. A strategy such as a KWHL (What do we *know*? What do we *want* to know? *How* do we find out? and finally, What have we *learned*?) is often used as an advance organizer (see Figure 3.9 and www.ncsu.edu/midlink/KWL.chart.html).

What do we *know*?	What do we *want* to know?	*How* will we find out?	What have we *learned*?

Figure 3.9   The KWHL Routine

Note: The "H" in the KWL was introduced by Dr. Mary Beth Dennis and first presented at a national meeting: Christensen, L. M., & Dennis, M. B. (1996, November). *Student-designed rubrics in the social studies: Fostering evaluative connoisseurship in the classroom.* National Council for The Social Studies, Washington, D.C.

Students record information in the first three columns. They then decide how to find the information they "want to know." This is one of a number of methods (see Chapter 5) to begin a process of exploration. It is frequently enacted by dividing students into smaller, self-selected interest groups to research topics of common student interest.

In this phase many multisensory instructional strategies are used. For instance, if one group is interested in a particular type of sea life, a guest speaker expert may be invited to speak on the topic. Students may create learning centers on what they have learned thus far. Videos and the Internet may enhance knowledge construction. Books, especially nonfiction, and the Internet may serve as valuable resources for information on the topics of interest. Field trips may enhance knowledge construction. Incorporating aesthetics as resources can be implemented to build knowledge on students' areas of research. This phase of the lesson can take a day or days, or weeks, according to the extent of the subject matter, and the range of standards incorporated. The first set of activities thus focuses on gathering or acquiring more information—the "Look" part of the development phase (see Figure 3.10).

As they acquire more information, students commence processing it; sorting and selecting materials; and reflecting on what it tells them, questioning, and organizing what they accumulate into a coherent set of ideas, concepts, or issues—the "Think" part of the process (see Figure 3.10). Relationships between different pieces of information are made through data processing, reasoning, and documentation (Sunal & Haas, 2008). Student questions are resolved through the multiple means described above. Often the teacher will provide examples and nonexamples of concepts to better clarify conceptions (Sunal & Haas, 2008).

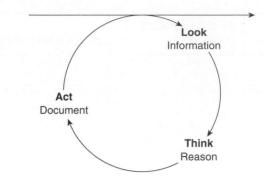

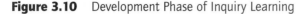

Figure 3.10   Development Phase of Inquiry Learning

Closure also occurs in this phase. This takes the form of an explanation embedded within an activity—the "Act" part of the development phase (see Figure 3.10). For example, students in the development phase practice the skill, concept, or generalization with guidance. This phase is guided practice. For instance, students may create a PowerPoint presentation, or a model, a poem, a collage, a rap, or a diorama as guided practice about the skill, concept, or generalization of study. The outcome is a piece of formative assessment.

Students will thus engage activities that enable them to:

Acquire information (Look). Teacher provides multisensory learning strategies to extend student exploration and learning—presentations, guest speakers, demonstrations, field trips, books, Internet searches, and so on. Students listen, search, and record.

Reason (Think). Students develop concepts and skills by working with and thinking about new concepts and information.

Document (Act). Students demonstrate their learning by documenting it using presentations, papers, brochures, newspaper articles, poems, songs, art, collages, and so on.

Phase 3: EXPANSION—Reviewing, Reflecting, Applying, and Assessing

Teachers assist students to apply knowledge and skills in new and different ways, solving problems, devising new applications, and refining skills. Students demonstrate what they have learned through documented means or artifacts.

Students expand on their knowledge constructions in this final phase of learning. They first review what they have learned—the "Look" part of the expansion phase, and then are guided by the teacher through a process of reflection and clarification—the "Think" part of the expansion phase (see Figure 3.11). Finally, the

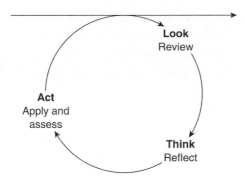

Figure 3.11   Expansion Phase of Inquiry Learning

students demonstrate their proficiency by applying what they have learned—the "Act" part of the expansion phase (see Figure 3.11).

Often these processes are applied through a medium that can be documented by a nontraditional means of assessment with an accompanying assessment rubric. Often teachers create rubrics, but students may also design their own. The list of types of assessment is not exhaustive and may take many forms—stories created to make a class book, a mosaic made up of major concepts of the topic studied, and so on (see pp. 108–110 in Chapter 5).

This phase is applied in nature, so the key is to have a meaningful independent activity where the teacher assists students to achieve final practice of a concept, skill, or generalization (Sunal & Haas, 2008). Once all of the artifacts are complete, then a whole class session of sharing and reflecting on what was learned occurs. This enables the teacher to evaluate the overall success of the lesson—the strengths and weaknesses of class learning—and to note areas requiring remediation or additional work.

Closure, as part of this final step in the lesson plan, engages the students in reflecting on the completed projects. The entire group of learners, including the teacher, reflects on the documented learning artifacts, providing the opportunity to ask, "Where do we go next?" It is almost like saying, "So what?" What do we want to learn now that we know this? This is a more summative form of assessment in which the final outcomes of the learning process are demonstrated. Additionally, the *closure* portion of the learning cycle lesson plan serves as the connecting phase in which students take what they have learned and inform others.

In the expansion phase, students will:

Review (Look). Students review the work produced in previous phases.

Reflect (Think). Teachers guide students through a process of reflection, asking questions, seeking clarification, providing feedback.

Apply and assess (Act). Students apply what they have learned, employing concepts and skills to solve problems, or using them in new and different ways. They demonstrate their proficiency by presenting a display and commenting on their work. The teacher assesses student work (performance) using an assessment rubric or scoring guide.

CASE EXAMPLE 3.2: THE ARTWORK OF JACOB LAWRENCE

The teacher planned a lesson using the frameworks/scaffolds previously described:

Look: She *reviewed instructional elements*—student prior knowledge, student capacities, state standards, community context, teaching materials, and learning resources.

Think: She selected *lesson components* from the large number of possible standards, outcomes, content, instructional strategies, learning activities, and assessment procedures.

Act: She organized a *lesson plan* using an organizing framework that includes standards, outcomes, preparation, presentation, and practice.

The following lesson plan illustrates the outcomes of these procedures for an inquiry learning lesson. Although cycles of teaching and learning do not always neatly fit the Look–Think–Act steps, they provide the means to distinguish between the forms of activity most closely related to the different levels and types of educational objective—*look:* acquiring knowledge; *think:* comprehension and analysis; *act:* using, applying, synthesizing, or evaluating.

Lesson: Inquiry Into the Artwork of Jacob Lawrence

Grade Level/Subject: 3rd–5th Grades

Duration: 4 class periods

STATE STANDARDS
Objectives and outcomes are drawn from the following Alabama State standards:

Alabama Standards: 3rd Grade
6. Identify conflicts involving use of land, economic competition for scarce resources, different political views, boundary disputes, and cultural differences within and between different geographic areas.

10. Describe characteristics and migration patterns of human populations in the Western Hemisphere.

Alabama Standards: 4th Grade

6. Identify cultural, economic, and political aspects of the lifestyles of early 19th-century farmers, plantation owners, slaves, and townspeople.

10. Describe significant social and educational changes in Alabama during the late 19th and early 20th centuries.

Alabama Standards: 5th Grade

13. Identify social, political, and economic changes that occurred during Reconstruction.

Special Needs Modifications: One-on-one instruction if necessary, peer tutors, provide step-by-step instructions, have appropriate reading materials, check on progress regularly, have an aide and assistive technology if possible, work with a special educator to modify instruction

Bilingual English Language Learner Strategies: Peer tutors; labels in student(s)' language; word walls in native tongue and English; adapted texts; instructions and directions in representative/native language if possible; utilization of visuals such as pictorial schematics, graphic organizers, charts to illustrate concepts, directions, and so on

Materials

Painting: *The Migration of the Negro Women* by Jacob Lawrence, from the Whitney Museum Web site (www.whitney.org/jacoblawrence/art/index.html)
Art journals

PHASE 1: EXPLORATION

Objectives/outcomes	Teacher instruction	Student learning	Assessment
Students will: Be able to make observations and develop generalizations related to cultural and political themes. **Outcomes** At the end of the lesson students will: Have an extended understanding of the social implications of art. Know how to answer higher order questions about art.	**Look** Download historical and cultural works of art by Jacob Lawrence from **www.whitney.org/ jacoblawrence/.** Ask students to note colors, shapes, patterns, textures, and cultural and/or political themes of the art piece. Ask them also to note any feelings that the work of art may generate.	**Look** Students examine the art of Jacob Lawrence. They note the colors, shapes, patterns, and themes in the pieces of art. They note any feelings the art may generate.	**Students will:** Write generalizations from group discussion in individual art journals about the artwork of Jacob Lawrence.

(Continued)

PHASE 1 (Continued)

Objectives/outcomes	Teacher instruction	Student learning	Assessment
Know how to achieve a cultural, historical, political, and geographical critical interpretation of artwork.	**Think** Ask students to examine and discuss the artwork by Jacob Lawrence and identify different cultural elements. Use overhead or large print of works of art for the class to observe. **Act** Teacher asks students to write the information that they discussed as generalizations from group in an art journal.	**Think** In groups of two or three, students examine the artwork of Southern black women by Jacob Lawrence from a print. Students will discuss the colors, shapes, patterns, themes, and feelings generated by the artwork in the group setting. **Act** Individually, students will write down colors, shapes, themes (political and cultural), and any feelings generated by observations.	

PHASE 2: DEVELOPMENT

Materials: www.whitney.org/jacoblawrence/art/women_work.html WebQuest on the Web site Text: Duggleby, J. (1998). *Story Painter: The Life of Jacob Lawrence* Info Section on the Web site above Art journals Maps Chart paper			
Objectives/outcomes	Teacher instruction	Student learning	Assessment
Students will: Revise their generalizations and observations about the work of art, the culture	**Look** The teacher will begin a discussion about the work and ask: • What is going on in this piece of art?	**Look** Students reexamine the artwork of Jacob Lawrence.	

Objectives/outcomes	Teacher instruction	Student learning	Assessment
embedded within, and any political meaning that they can report from varied print and nonprint formats.	• Who is in the artwork? • Who is not in it? • What are they doing? • What gender is the person doing the work? • What is the woman's skin color? • What can we tell about the person, objects, where the picture is located?	Students answer direct questions about the gender and gender role of the woman in the artwork.	
	Think The teacher asks students to examine the lines in the work: • What types of lines have been used? • Are the lines thick, thin, straight, curved, or wavy? • How are colors and textures used? • What do you think the artist may have been trying to tell us from this piece of art? • What might be the subject, theme, or intention of the artist?	**Think** Students think more carefully by critically examining Jacob Lawrence's artwork. Students all respond to teacher questions. Students think of five questions for the artist.	Five written questions in students' art journals. The teacher captures student responses on chart paper.
	Act The teacher asks students to write down five questions that they would like to ask Jacob Lawrence. The teacher writes down questions (in groups, or by the teacher on chart paper for ELL emergent writers). The teacher asks students to offer their interpretation of the work of art.	**Act** Students write five questions for the artist, Jacob Lawrence. Students share their questions to be written on chart paper for the entire class. Students offer some of their interpretations of the artwork.	

PHASE 2 (Continued)

Objectives/outcomes	Teacher instruction	Student learning	Assessment
	The teacher asks students to look at further examples of artwork depicting social and political themes and embedded messages.	Students look at other work in Jacob Lawrence's *Migration* series.	
	Teacher asks students to complete the WebQuest at www.whitney.org/jacoblawrence/art/women_work.html.	Students complete the WebQuest online about Jacob Lawrence in pairs.	Students' Web-Quest outcomes.
	Teacher asks students to read the "Info" section on the Web site that describes the life of black women depicted in his work.	Students read the "Info" box on the front page of the Web site that describes Lawrence's interpretation of the context and political climate of women.	Students read the "Info" box on the Web site to the teacher.
	Teacher brings students together in a whole group for reading.		
	The teacher reads children's literature on the life of Jacob Lawrence, *Story Painter: The Life of Jacob Lawrence.*		
	The teacher discusses where he is from. Use maps for students to show the place of Harlem in comparison to where students live.	Students use maps to locate Harlem, NY, and their location. They may want to take note of mileage.	
	Teacher asks students to compare their heritage to that of Jacob Lawrence in their art journals.	Students write their individual comparisons of how their cultural heritage in 2009 differs from that of Jacob Lawrence in their art journals.	Students' written comparison indicating revised generalizations.

PHASE 3: EXPANSION

Materials:

Paper or chart paper, crayons, markers, colored pencils, paints.
Directions for (diamante, a Haiku, or acrostic) poetry

Objectives/outcomes	Teacher instruction	Student learning	Assessment
Students will: Apply their generalizations and observations about one of Jacob Lawrence's works by writing a piece of poetry and illustrating it.	**Look** Teacher asks students to represent their ideas about freedom in a way that Jacob Lawrence did.	**Look** Students will reexamine the artwork of Jacob Lawrence to decide how they wish to represent their ideas. Students decide which medium they wish to use to portray their ideas.	
	Think Teacher asks students to identify the colors, objects, and people that they wish to put into their artwork.	**Think** Students will decide which types of lines, people, objects, and colors that they want to use.	
	Teacher asks students to individually draw their own artwork as a rendition of a Jacob Lawrence piece of art and give it a title.	**Act** Students will complete their artwork individually.	Art work and poetry accomplished by applied generalizations from the study of Jacob Lawrence.
	Teacher asks students to write poetry (diamante, a Haiku, or acrostic) to emphasize the work of art.	Students will write a type of poetry to accompany their work of art.	
	Display the students' artwork and poetry on a bulletin board.		
	Have students take digital pictures of their works of art and poetry to share, either in a school-to-home communication or classroom newsletter.	Students take digital photos of their work for a class display.	Teacher and students discuss features of the art and poetry. They assess the quality of those features.

CONCLUSION

This chapter has focused on lesson planning, showing how teachers use continuing cycles of an action research routine to assist them to keep track of the diverse issues that need to be taken into account as they construct a program of learning for their students. The simple Look–Think–Act process is applied to direct instruction and inquiry learning lessons. It provides the means by which teachers can take into account the wide array of elements that need to be incorporated into their students' program of learning, and enhances their professional capacities and feelings of personal satisfaction.

LEARNING RESOURCES

Reflection

1. Prepare a lesson of your choice, either direct instruction or inquiry, applying the Look–Think–Act cycle for each phase of the lesson as demonstrated in this chapter.

2. Think aloud and note down your own thoughts as you work through the process of constructing your lesson.

3. Upon completion, read through the notes you kept as you developed your lesson. What is significant? Your own learning? Confusion? Ah-has? Comments on the process? Other?

4. Identify the key issues from those you noted. Share these with the class. Have them comment on the issues.

5. How does the Look–Think–Act cycle affect the way you plan your lessons? What do you know now about lesson planning that you did not know?

6. **Look**: Using the "Look" part of the lesson planning framework (with students' assistance, if possible) identify:

   - The instructional elements you will consider

   - How you will access the necessary information

   - How you will use it to construct an effective plan

   - The basis for making sound decisions about issues affecting student learning

   Think: How will you utilize the parts of planning to focus precisely on issues and strategies to cultivate the students' learning needs?

   Act: Working with your students, describe some modes of assessment (don't forget about nontraditional means of assessment) to assess student learning. Have students assist you in developing rubrics to document the standards and objectives they have achieved.

Web Sites

Jacob Lawrence:

www.whitney.org/jacoblawrence/

Here you will find a treasure of resources about Jacob Lawrence and related art information for classroom use, including a biography and a WebQuest.

The Learning Cycle:

www.learnnc.org/lp/pages/learningcycle

This is just one of countless Web sites about the learning cycle.

Learning Cycle Diagram:

www.sasked.gov.sk.ca/docs/tensoc/activity/cycle.html

This provides a diagram that clearly explains the nature of the learning cycle.

U.S. State Standards:

www.edstandards.org/StSu/Social.html

This site provide links to Web sites for state standards for each U.S. state.

Mary Haas, PhD, Professor at WVU:

www.hre.wvu.edu/mhaas/spring2006/acourtney/

As a social studies professor, Dr. Mary Haas is a strong proponent of the learning cycle. At this site, one of her students has created a rubric for a WebQuest about economics.

Children, Online Learning, and Authentic Teaching Skills in Primary Education:

www.educ.utas.edu.au/users/ilwebb/Research/action_learning.htm

This Web site describes the original action learning processes suggested by Reg Levens.

ALEX – Alabama Learning Exchange:

http://alex.state.al.us/index.php

This site stores all of the Alabama state standards for each grade level and content area. In addition, there are lesson plans, links, professional development opportunities, and more.

Action Research and Action Learning:

www.scu.edu.au/schools/gcm/ar/arp/actlearn.html

Bob Dick provides a clear description of the relationship between action research and action learning.

Additional Reading

Action Learning: Research & Practice (Journal). Abingdon, UK: Taylor & Francis.

Sunal, C. S., & Haas, M. E. (2008). *Social studies for the elementary and middle grades: A constructivist approach.* Boston, MA: Allyn & Bacon.

NOTES

1. See Chapter 6 for a more extended treatment of assessment procedures.

2. The second of the two lessons is presented in Chapter 4.

3. Chapter 5 explores a cycle of action learning that is applied to each of the phases of inquiry learning.

Instruction

Facilitating Student Learning

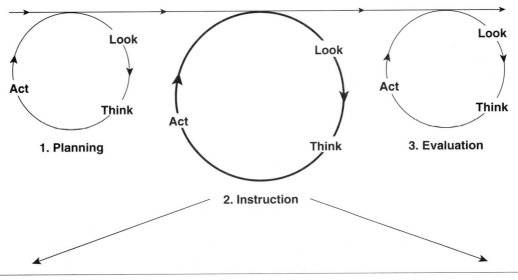

Instruction Phase

This chapter uses an action research routine to assist teachers to keep track of the complex processes of instruction. It first describes three central issues that need to be taken into account as teachers instruct their students:

- **Student engagement:** Suggesting how to move students from an attitude of *resistance and apathy* to one of *interest and excitement*

- **Prior knowledge:** Identifying what students know and can do, derived from their *natural capacities* and their *socially learned knowledge*

- **Domains of knowledge:** Describing the *cognitive, affective, and psychomotor* objectives to be incorporated into lessons

It then shows how the Look–Think–Act action research routine can assist teachers to enhance their instruction:

- *Observing* student activities and performance—observing and talking (Look)

- *Checking* student activities and performance—analyzing and assessing (Think)

- *Affirming* or *remediating* student learning through reinforcing comments, repeating instructions and demonstrations, and celebrating success (Act)

ACCOMPLISHING EFFECTIVE INSTRUCTION

Previous chapters described how an action research framework can assist teachers to plan more effective instruction and learning that take into account the diverse characteristics and qualities of their students (Chapter 1), and the multidimensional nature of learning processes (see Chapter 2). Action research, we suggested, provides the means by which teachers can systematically engage these issues and assist their students to attain the standards on which the lesson focuses.

The following sections extend our exploration of these issues, examining some of the basic conditions needed to achieve effective student learning: *student engagement*—finding ways to capture the interest and attention of our students, and *prior learning*—starting with what students already know or can do. We also investigate the *types or domains of knowledge and skill* that students need to acquire as part of their education. Learning, we discover, is much more than memorizing a fixed body of information, but the dynamic acquisition of a wide range of different types of knowledge and skills. Finally, we describe how action research processes assist teachers to take these issues into account as they engage in the demanding but rewarding act of teaching.

CONDITIONS OF LEARNING (1): STUDENT ENGAGEMENT

It is a joy to be in a classroom where students excitedly and enthusiastically engage their work and express clear satisfaction in their accomplishments. The energy and fulfillment evident in this type of context is gratifying to teachers and students alike. The reverse is also sometimes true in contexts where teachers experience groups of students that are sullen, disrespectful, and argumentative, and classroom work becomes a daily grind for all concerned. One of the principal tasks in teaching is to generate a positive orientation in students that enables them to invest themselves in classroom activities and find satisfaction in the outcomes of their endeavors.

As they work through each lesson, therefore, teachers need to be constantly aware of the demeanor of their students and to gauge the extent to which they are actively involved in classroom activities. They will be able to do so by assessing the degree of interest and involvement students express through their actions, behaviors, and responses, and to plan and modify their lessons accordingly.

EXPERIENCING STUDENT ENGAGEMENT

The levels of student engagement are clearly illustrated by my experience with a particular social studies lesson. On one occasion, following a discussion about people in poverty being always on "the take," I had my students fill out the forms to apply for food stamps. Coming from privileged backgrounds, they had no experience in these matters.

They worked busily, some *excited* by the activity, and most were at least *interested* in the project. Soon, however, their busyness turned to arguing and almost every group was in turmoil. Although they were willing to work on the task at hand, I had not planned well enough for them to accomplish it, and the situation became unpleasant to say the least, with some children becoming quite *resistant* to the activity. We worked it out and muddled through, but many of the children became *apathetic,* and refused to engage in discussions about the issue.

The next year, I was determined to try the lesson once again with a new group of students. This time when teaching the lesson, I assigned class members to a "family" group, and though they became more interested, they were still a bit guarded. All of the important documentation necessary to complete the forms was provided. The student groups just had to locate the information and place it in the correct lines in order to qualify for food stamps. They were motivated to prove me wrong in suggesting that it was difficult to get food stamps. The lesson went off without a hitch, the students being *excited* and engaged for the entire 50-minute lesson, certain that their "family" would qualify for food stamps.

I turned the paperwork over to a local social worker who discovered only one out of the five "family" groups had filled out the forms correctly. It was a great lesson for them about how difficult it is to qualify for food stamps. Surprisingly, for me, the students became quite *apathetic* and resentful, and I was at a loss to understand their responses. Following another discussion, I suggested that maybe the social worker could visit our class, but that was a complete "bomb"!! They had no interest in having someone from the community coming in to "determine how incompetent they were in following directions on food stamp forms." I never dreamed that I would meet such *resistance.* I finally was able to convince my class of the benefit of a session with the social worker, who visited them and answered their predeveloped questions about their failure to receive food stamps.

Upon reflection I saw the errors I had made. Although well-intended, my instruction was not well thought out, and the method of instruction, materials, planning, and implementation needed lots of tweaking to keep the 35 fifth-grade students interested or excited, rather than providing an experience that generated apathy and resistance.

—L.C.

A student's orientation to school is considerably affected by his or her history of experience. If students have experienced consistent failure, or have low expectations of themselves due to the influence of family and peers, then teachers need to find ways to provide them with positive experiences that tell them, "You are a clever and interesting person." In this way teachers can overcome messages from past experience and engage the interests and experiences of students. One of the purposes of engaging action research in our teaching is to enable us to acquire and accumulate a body of knowledge about our students that assists us to understand their world, and to therefore be in a position to provide appropriate learning activities and processes.

Through continuing processes of inquiry we can get to know our students—what "turns them on"—in a much more systematic and comprehensive fashion. When we do so, we are in a position to regularly engage our students at the highest levels of the engagement, at a minimum ensuring a level of interest that enables them to produce good learning outcomes, and to reach the highest level—Excitement—on a regular basis. It's the difference between one parent's comment, "Amanda can't wait to come to school, every day!" and another's, "It is just so hard to get James to school in the morning. I just about have to drag him out of the house."

The Index of Engagement (Figure 4.1) suggests the different ways that students are affected by the environment and activities of the classroom. The responses of children engaged at the highest level—Excitement—clearly show their orientation to their work. They animatedly volunteer information; speak enthusiastically; eagerly share their work with others; are smiling, cheerful, and positive; sustain active engagement in their work over extended periods; express great satisfaction; and produce high-quality work. Students at the next level—Interest—are still working well, volunteering information, and speaking about their work. They work cooperatively, are businesslike, are actively engaged, and express satisfaction with the quality of work they produce.

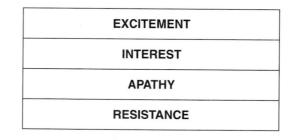

Figure 4.1   Index of Engagement

The degree of engagement of these students contrasts markedly to those at the next level—Apathy. When students are in this frame of mind, they are merely "going through a routine," their intent clearly being to "get through the day" or "give the teacher what she wants." They provide limited responses to inquiries or suggestions, speak and act lethargically, are disinterested, engage learning tasks in limited fashion, and express little satisfaction in their work, which is often of marginal quality. In the worst case they may become "Resistant," refusing to respond to teacher questions, suggestions, or directives; being challenging and disrespectful; engaging in uncooperative or disruptive behavior; being surly or angry; engaging their work in tokenistic fashion; expressing overt disinterest; and producing very poor quality work.[1]

One of the major purposes of the processes described in this book is to assist teachers to identify ways they can move their students "up the ladder" of this index. The following chapters suggest some ways in which teachers can provide students with learning activities that engage their interest, but the major way this happens is for us to figuratively get into the minds of the students, envisioning the types of events and activities that excite their attention and link with the world they know. Though there are clearly times when teachers need to direct misbehaving students to focus on their studies, a consistent default to threats or directives signals the need to rethink the lesson.

As the following section suggests, a fundamental strategy is to link the activities in the lesson to events and experiences grounded in the students' life worlds. The lesson on the artwork of Jacob Lawrence, for instance (see Chapter 3, p. 54), used guest speakers, visits, and a variety of other activities to actively link the children to the subject matter. The Community Commercial Project lesson (see Appendix, p. 154) likewise engages the students directly in explorations and activities related to their local community. Engagement is not something that is achieved separately, and though often an important feature of the first stages of a lesson, it is accomplished in an ongoing way throughout the activities and events comprising classroom life.

CONDITIONS OF LEARNING (2): PRIOR KNOWLEDGE— WHAT STUDENTS KNOW AND CAN DO

The need to frame teaching within a process of inquiry also becomes evident when we consider the nature of the learning process. Two fundamental conditions provide the very foundations of the process of learning and instruction—what students know and what they can do. These fundamentals can be encapsulated in the simple statements:

Start with what students KNOW. Work with what they can DO.

What students have learned in school comprises but a small fraction of what students KNOW. What they KNOW comes from a long history of learning and experiences in their family and community contexts, and from diverse other sources including the media and experiences in travel or visits to other towns, cities, communities, and sometimes countries. The extensive corpus of knowledge that "comes through the door" with every child provides a rich resource from which rich learning experiences can derive.

What a student can DO likewise encompasses a much wider range of capabilities than is measured or recorded in school tests and achievement records. It encompasses all the skills that students acquire in the first years of their lives and in consequent life in their family and community. This may cover a wide range of skills that may not be evident within a classroom environment, but that have the potential to greatly extend the possibilities open to the teacher.

Diversity in Student Capabilities and Capacities

Any group will include students with widely divergent natural levels of ability and comprise individuals at quite different stages of development. If we ask them to engage in activities they have not the capacity to accomplish, we set them up for failure. Conversely, if we fail to provide opportunities for them to make full use of their skills and capacities, their learning will be stunted, and their potentials unrealized. A group is likely to include individuals with highly developed artistic skills and others who struggle to draw a straight line with a rule; some who are highly adept in the sports field and others who bumble and bungle their way through the simplest physical task; some who engage in highly mature modes of conversation and others who converse in a childlike manner. Some of this results from their history of experience, but their natural abilities also play an important role in what a student can and cannot do.

Gardner's (1999) work on multiple intelligences alerts us to the many capacities and capabilities that can be used in learning. He suggests that different students have different strengths and learn in different ways, engaging linguistic, logical, spatial/visual, musical, kinesthetic, interpersonal, intrapersonal, and naturalistic intelligences in the process of learning. When we take advantage of these multiple intelligences, we increase the learning potentials of our students, and open up the possibilities and potentials that are in them all.

Student diversity is therefore a common artifact of everyday classroom life, but it is sometimes manifest in students whose capacities—physical, emotional, and intellectual—are so dramatically different from others that they are classified as special needs students. As indicated in all lesson plans, specific strategies may be needed to accommodate those whose capacities do not fit the norm. This is as true for those who are linguistically different—who have limited understanding of the standard classroom language—as for those with particular physical, emotional, or intellectual impairments, though the former may be chronic conditions.

What a Child Knows and Can Do: Family and Community Experiences

An extensive and powerful body of research on educational achievement stretching back more than 50 years (e.g., Coleman et al., 1966; Jencks et al., 1972) shows clearly that factors related to the family and community have a much greater effect on academic achievement. So clear is this connection that it is now accepted as a given in the educational research literature. What it suggests is that classroom activities that fail to take account of students' family and community environments are likely to have less chance of enabling them to successfully achieve the academic goals of the school. Only by starting with what the child knows and can do, not just in the limited sense of a pretest of discrete lesson content, but across all areas of intelligence, can a teacher provide the means by which students can connect with the activities and events in the classroom—to move from the known to the unknown.

A major purpose of the action research routines embedded in these pages is to provide the means to reveal the students' tacit knowledge—knowledge often unspoken and of which individuals may not be consciously aware—and to use that as an important feature of the lesson. Providing students with opportunities to reveal and further explore their own experience supplies a resource that enriches the learning experience and provides a basis for higher levels of engagement.

The need to start with "what the students know" is evident in all lessons, but is a particular focus of action learning/inquiry learning approaches to instruction (see, e.g., "The Artwork of Jacob Lawrence" in Chapter 3 on p. 54, and the Appendix). As the following narrative—"A Community Commercial"—suggests, teaching is much more than providing students with a fixed body of knowledge to memorize. It is a process of using the students' knowledge of their own locality to construct highly engaging and creative learning experiences that provide students with a richly rewarding education.

A COMMUNITY COMMERCIAL

The Appendix incorporates a lesson plan for a group of middle school students from Aston Point, an urban community in New Jersey. Needing to engage students in an oral history project, the teacher discovered through her initial investigation that the students were dissatisfied with the condition of their community and wished to do something about it. By assisting students to reflect on the possibilities open to them, the teacher enabled them to identify what was good about their community and what it had to offer. Through ongoing processes of inquiry, they not only identified these features of their community, but also decided to make a "commercial." They engaged in a wide range of diverse learning activities in order to write a script, videotape appropriate material,

(Continued)

(Continued)

and produce a video. Their interest and enthusiasm enabled them to complete a video that was shown to an audience of students, teachers, parents, and community members, and was applauded by all. The wide range of learning objectives they accomplished in the process was testament to the educational potential that exists in every community.

—S.B.

Understanding and Using Student Knowledge and Experience

Teachers therefore need to accumulate a body of knowledge and understanding of the multiple dimensions of their students. If they assume that their own "body of knowledge," or understandings, can provide a sufficient basis for their students' learning, if they fail to capitalize on the richly diverse knowledge that derives from their students' history of experience, then they will fail to fulfill the learning potentials that are in every classroom. Teachers need, in other words, to engage in ongoing "research" to engage the body of understanding that enables them to successfully accomplish the rewarding task of facilitating their students' learning.

If we are to ground their learning in "what is known," then we have much to learn to ensure that our classrooms are interesting, engaging, and productive learning contexts for our students.

Fortunately, we have a range of resources that can assist us in this process of learning. While the students themselves provide a wonderful source of information, parents, community members, media, literature, and many other sources provide the means to engage the world of the students we serve. We also have a body of information in school records that provide indications—test results, past reports, and so on—that enable us to build a picture of the capabilities and past performance of each student.

The following activities provide just a few of the ways in which teachers can start to build an understanding of their students. They involve activities that take them out of the classroom, and may require them to take extra time outside of the school schedule, but the rewards for doing so far exceed the relatively small investment required. Teachers may:

- Talk about the local community in class, ask questions about it, and provide opportunities for students to recount stories of family and community events.

- Ask some students to take them for a short tour of their neighborhood.

- Meet small groups of students for a soda in a local fast food establishment.

- Take small groups of students for short excursions to interesting places or events in the area—a concert in the park, an exhibition or display in a local venue.

- Visit students at home to meet parents and siblings.

Each of these types of activity not only enables teachers to gain a greater understanding of their students, but provides rich material to incorporate into classroom learning activities. As they enter family and community life worlds, teachers also learn to understand their students in a richly meaningful way, and in the process develop relationships that enable them to accomplish their work more effectively. Action research and action learning routines enable both teachers and students to reveal these rich potentials and to incorporate them into teaching/learning processes. As Figure 4.2 indicates, they provide the means for teachers to reveal the strengths within each student—what they know and can do, and to use them to move into the unknown—what they must learn.

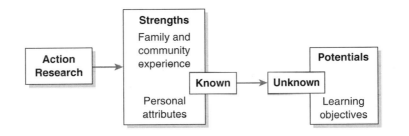

Figure 4.2   Using What Students Know and Can Do

CONTENT OF THE CURRICULUM: DOMAINS OF KNOWLEDGE

Any curriculum includes a multitude of elements that signal the wide array of skills and knowledge teachers must assist their students to learn. This diversity, however, is not just a random array of information and behaviors, but a carefully organized body of knowledge that can be systematically developed as students move through their schooling. As described in Chapter 1, Bloom, Krathwohl, and their colleagues described a taxonomy containing three *domains* that provide us with the means to keep track of the distinct types of knowledge and skills our students need to acquire—the cognitive domain that focuses on intellectual skills, the affective domain that relates to feelings or emotional orientations, and the psychomotor domain concerned with physical skills and attributes.

Taxonomy of Educational Objectives: The Cognitive Domain

Chapter 1 signaled the diverse array of knowledge and skills that comprises any school curriculum, indicating the diverse elements that need to be incorporated into any lesson. The diverse nature of student learning is signaled in the terminologies (verbs) used to describe learning outcomes and learning activities. Bloom and Krathwohl's taxonomy of educational objectives (1956) thus includes the following terms:

- **Knowledge:** Define, recall, recognize, remember, label, list, name, reproduce

- **Comprehension:** Grasp (the meaning), compare, contrast, rephrase, explain, restate, give examples

- **Application:** Apply, use, employ, utilize, implement, produce, report, show, write, solve, develop, predict, illustrate

- **Analysis:** Break down, categorize, arrange, compare, correlate, differentiate, distinguish, prioritize, infer, separate, subdivide, conclude, determine

- **Synthesis:** Adapt, combine, compose, create, devise, produce, design, develop, construct, incorporate, integrate plan, structure

- **Evaluation:** Judge, evaluate, appraise, compare, conclude, justify, assess, critique, decide (the merit)

A classroom lesson that requires students to remember discrete pieces of information—What is the capital of Illinois?—requires the student to *remember* that fact and to be able to reproduce it at a later time. The student then can be said to "know" that information merely by responding "Springfield" to that question. To demonstrate that she understands or *comprehends,* however, the student would need to explain what is meant by the word "capital," providing evidence that she understood it in terms of a "seat of government" and thus demonstrated that she "knew" the significance of that statement. Further indications of the extent of the student's level of comprehension would require a more extended set of learning activities that required the student to present evidence that she could differentiate a capital from other important centers (e.g., industrial, commercial)—*application, analysis.* Given the requirement to describe a hypothetical state, she would be able to incorporate a capital and its operation appropriately—*synthesis*—and assess the merits or adequacy of different capitals.

The teacher's task, in this process, is to provide a sufficiently diverse range of learning tasks to ensure that students accomplish all of the domains that are signaled in the state standards. The teacher would not only provide generative questions that would elicit the different forms of knowledge, but also provide activities that would enable students to learn and demonstrate that they had acquired the different forms of knowledge incorporated into the standards.

The lesson plans incorporated into the chapters and the Appendix provide many examples of the different questions and activities teachers use to accomplish these tasks. The persuasive speaking lesson at the end of this chapter (p. 83), for instance, provides examples of the questions used by the teacher:

How do your friends try to convince you about something?

What makes their argument effective?

What speeches have you heard recently to persuade you to take a particular point of view on an issue?

What did the speaker do that made his or her speech persuasive?

These not only require students to remember events, but to understand, analyze, synthesize, apply, and evaluate. Further activities within the lesson enable students to reinforce and extend the different forms of knowledge they acquire about the topic in question, and to demonstrate their levels of proficiency with regard to the state standards around which the lesson is centered. A good example of the relationship between objectives and standards is found on p. 141 of the Appendix, Case Example A.1— the lesson on sea life.

Anderson and Krathwohl (2001) have recently suggested an enhanced taxonomy that distinguishes the different domains of knowledge from the cognitive processes required to attain them. Their schema envisages knowledge in four domains:

- **Factual knowledge:** Knowledge of terminology, specific details, and elements

- **Conceptual knowledge:** Knowledge of classifications and categories; of principals and generalizations; of theories, models, and structures

- **Procedural knowledge:** Knowledge of subject-specific skills and algorithms; of subject-specific techniques and methods; and of criteria for determining choice of procedures

- **Metacognitive knowledge:** Awareness and knowledge of one's own cognition— strategic knowledge, cognitive tasks, and self-knowledge

The cognitive processes required to acquire these forms of knowledge include the ability to:

- **Remember:** Recognizing, recalling

- **Understand:** Interpreting, exemplifying, classifying, summarizing, inferring, comparing, and explaining

- **Apply:** Executing, implementing

- **Analyze:** Differentiating, organizing, attributing

- **Evaluate:** Checking, critiquing

- **Create:** Generating, planning, producing

Anderson and Krathwohl (2001) suggest that we can keep track of these different elements by placing them in a taxonomy table (see Table 4.1) that enables us to check that, over time, the educational objectives in our lessons will cover the full range of types of knowledge and cognitive processes:

Knowledge dimension	Cognitive process dimension					
	Remember	Understand	Apply	Analyze	Evaluate	Create
Factual knowledge		Obj 1.3				
Conceptual knowledge			Obj 1.3.1			
Procedural knowledge			Obj 1.3.2			
Metacognitive knowledge				Obj 1.4.1		

Table 4.1   Taxonomy Table of Educational Objectives

According to this schema, lesson plans should incorporate learning processes that enable students to acquire the different forms of knowledge and cognitive skills required to attain the standards on which a lesson focuses. These more sophisticated processes of learning provide students with the means to acquire the comprehensive body of knowledge and skills that will enable them to navigate the increasingly complex social worlds they face in this 21st century.

Taxonomy of Educational Objectives:
The Affective Domain

The affective domain is concerned about the *feelings* or *emotional orientation* an individual has toward people, events, activities, objects, or places. The affective dimension is a key determinant of behavior, the way people *feel* about issues and events largely determining the way they respond and behave. This contrasts with the cognitive domain that focuses on the way people *think* about issues. When students are learning, they are not only learning the content of a lesson, they are also acquiring attitudes, opinions, appreciations, values, and interests. The purpose of teaching is therefore not only to enable students to acquire information and skills, but also to ensure that the learner acquires appropriate attitudes and values. When students learn about cultural difference, for instance, we are not just teaching them the facts of cultural difference, but assisting them to learn that different lifestyles and ways of living are OK. When we teach them reading, we not only provide them with the skills, but also seek to give them a positive orientation toward literacy.

As teachers plan and implement their lessons, therefore, they need to incorporate activities and events that provide an appropriate emotional orientation toward the content of the lesson. Krathwohl and his colleagues (1964) have suggested a taxonomy that maps out the different types of emotional orientation that can be included in any set of educational objectives. These suggest that lessons should incorporate questions, activities, and interactions that enable students to develop the following capacities:

- **Receiving:** Being aware of or attending to something. A teacher would be aware of whether the student is focused on the learning activities being engaged. Behavioral terms associated with this domain include: looks, watches, listens, accepts, identifies, and so on.

- **Responding:** Actively participating, attending to events, and reacting appropriately to stimuli. Behavioral terms include: participates, responds, volunteers, obeys, answers, shows interest, enjoys, performs, presents, reports, and so on.

- **Valuing:** Attaching worth to particular ideas, objects, behaviors, or other phenomena, ranging from acceptance to commitment. Students demonstrate values through their actions and their words. Teachers present learning activities to assist students reveal and develop their values. Behavioral terms associated with this domain include: believes, values, supports, appreciates, shows concern, demonstrates, justifies, proposes, shares, and so on.

- **Organization (of value complex):** Building an internally consistent values system. Learners compare different values, resolve conflicts among them, and develop a personal philosophy. They recognize the need for balance, think systematically in solving problems, and accept responsibility for their own behavior. Behavioral terms include: arranges, combines, compares, integrates, modifies, organizes, generalizes, commits, and so on.

- **Characterization (by a value or value complex):** Acting consistently according to a set of internalized values. Behavior is consistent and predictable. Behavioral terms include: displays self-reliance and appropriate personal, social, and emotional adjustment; works independently; maintains good habits; and so on.

This taxonomy is hierarchical (Figure 4.3), so that the early years of schooling will be on attributes within the lower levels of the taxonomy—receiving, responding, and valuing, with increasing emphasis being placed on organization and characterization in the higher grades.

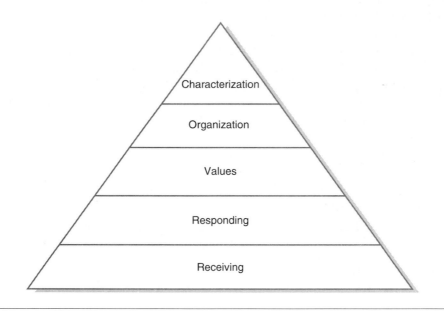

Figure 4.3   Taxonomy of Educational Objectives: The Affective Domain

Taxonomy of Educational Objectives: The Psychomotor Domain

A school curriculum is concerned not only with development of intellectual and emotional capacities, but also with the physical attributes a person needs to acquire or enhance in the course of their education. Psychomotor attributes are therefore important in areas such as speech development, reading, writing, physical education, artistic performances, and so on. The psychomotor domain presented by Harrow (1972) describes the development of physical attributes and capacities:

- **Reflex movement:** Reactions that are not learned, for example, response to pain

- **Fundamental movements:** Basic movements such as walking, grasping, nodding, sitting, standing, and so on

- **Perception:** Response to stimuli, for example, visual, auditory, kinesthetic, tactile discrimination

- **Physical abilities:** Strength, agility, flexibility, endurance, and so on

- **Skilled movements:** Advanced abilities and complex movements required for sports, dance, acting, and so on

- **Nondiscursive communication:** Expressive and interpretive movements, including those incorporated into dancing and gymnastics, as well as body language in normal communication

General objectives associated with this domain include writing legibly, reproducing a picture or map, operating a machine or musical instrument, demonstrating correct posture, performing a dance routine, and so on. Behavioral terms include grips, makes, manipulates, builds, constructs, paints, hears, observes, draws, and so on. All suggest the types of objectives related to psychomotor functioning to be included in a lesson plan.

Lessons therefore need to incorporate activities that enable students to achieve standards related to the development or enhancement of physical attributes, and the accomplishing of tasks and performances requiring human movement, listening or observing, or sensing. In the Commercial Project, for instance (Appendix, p. 154), students practice the acting and presentation skills outlined in the Procedures column in order to achieve standards in speaking described in the Objectives/Outcomes and Standards columns.

USING ACTION LEARNING TO ACCOMPLISH DIVERSE LEARNING OUTCOMES

The use of action learning assists teachers to incorporate a broad range of learning activities that enable students to acquire the diverse forms of knowledge inherent in any set of standards. By characterizing the processes of learning in terms of systematic inquiry, teachers will move students past the rather limited routines of memorization and recall to actively engage the more exciting possibilities involved in processes of systematic inquiry. The diverse forms of knowledge and array of skills they learn will provide tools of investigation, analysis, and application that will stay with them for life.

We might envisage the Look–Think–Act sequence as encompassing the following domains of knowledge:

Look: Acquiring knowledge

Think: Acquiring and using skills of comprehension, application, analysis, and evaluation

Act: Acquiring capacities related to application, synthesis, creation, and performance

As teachers implement lessons, therefore, action research frameworks assist students to engage a variety of learning and assessment strategies to ensure comprehensive and effective learning that extends their capabilities and enables them to reach high levels of attainment.

USING ACTION RESEARCH TO ENHANCE INSTRUCTION

The beginning of the lesson is a time of anticipation, where teachers gain students' attention by informing them of the purposes and activities to come, and linking those to their past experiences and their interests. Often teachers will focus students' attention and put them in a receptive frame of mind by providing an "advance organizer"—an organizing framework of ideas or information—or asking questions that stimulate the students' imagination. In this initial phase of the lesson, the teacher will therefore:

- **Look:** Review the lesson plan and observe students to ensure their attention is focused

- **Think:** Select appropriate information and elicit questions

- **Act:** Use a variety of means to focus student attention—present information, demonstrate an activity, display a picture or video clip, ask eliciting questions, and so on

As the lesson proceeds, the teacher informs students about learning activities in which they will engage and tasks they must perform. Teachers use the Look–Think–Act routine to review the progress of the lesson, observe and assess student performance, and plan continuing steps to extend or remediate student learning.

INSTRUCTION: OBSERVING AND ASSESSING STUDENT LEARNING

As students engage in learning activities, teachers need to keep track of the multiple activities in which the class is engaged and the progress of each child. They must carefully observe students' work and evaluate their performance, identifying children who are not engaged, who are performing poorly, or who appear to misunderstand what they are supposed to be doing (LOOK). As they observe these events, they will consider the nature of problems students are experiencing (THINK) and what they need to do to take remedial action (ACT). This cyclical activity is repeated throughout a lesson till students accomplish desired outcomes and the objectives of the lesson are achieved.

An action research cycle assists teachers to systematically monitor student activity and progress (see Figure 4.4). Teachers will:

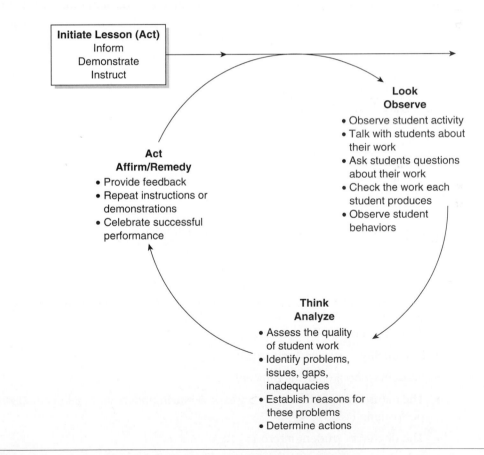

Figure 4.4   Instruction: Observing and Assessing Student Learning

- **Look:** Observe student activities, behavior, and performance
- **Think:** Identify the cause of inadequate performances or inappropriate behaviors or actions
- **Act:** Take action to affirm student learning, and remedy gaps or inadequacies in student performance

LOOK: Observing Student Activity, Performance, and Behavior

With so many students engaged in activity, teachers must constantly be alert to the nuances of action and behavior. They need to constantly be aware of what is happening, what the students are doing, and how well they are accomplishing their assigned activities. Even if the whole class is listening to a presentation or watching a video, the teacher must be aware of the ways in which students are engaging the activity—whether they are focusing on it, whether they understand it, whether they find it interesting, or whether they struggle to maintain their attention.

Observation is therefore one of the key tools of the teacher, enabling him or her to see what is happening and to roughly assess the progress of each student, or the quality of the student's work. Teachers need to be aware of the direct signals of poor behavior, but also to read the subtleties of nonverbal communication— body language—that signals "where students are at."

But observation is often insufficient, and teachers need to engage in conversations and discussions with students to ascertain the degree of understanding they have attained, or to understand why students are unable to perform adequately or appropriately.

Teachers will monitor student progress throughout a lesson, therefore, by:

Observing

Teachers will watch students perform assigned activities. They will note:

- The children who are "on task"
- The quality of student performance
- Students who are having difficulty
- The nature of the difficulties they experience in understanding information or performing tasks
- The degree of student interest
- The general behavior of students—engaged, disengaged, bored, restless, and so on

Asking Questions

Teachers ask questions to clarify the nature of student activities. They will:

- Ask questions that enable students to comment on their work

- Ask questions to assess student level of understanding of content or process

- Elicit and listen to student comments about their work

- Ask questions to push students' thinking boundaries

CHECKING STUDENT PROGRESS

In the first days of my practice teaching, I stood at the front of the class and observed the students engaged in activity. From time to time I would stop their activity and provide comment or clarifying instructions, based on my observations of what I could see of their work. When they had completed the work, I would give a short test or have them display their work so that I could assess their progress.

My mentor teacher suggested I note the way he monitored student activity. As they worked, he walked around the room, looking at their work as they sat at their desks, asking questions, and providing assessments or clarifying comments about the activity in which students were engaged. Sometimes he would have students stop their work and speak to the class, giving instructions or making comments that would clarify the activity in which they were engaged, or encouraging them to improve the quality of their work. The children usually were very responsive to his instruction as he spoke directly to issues or problems that were common to many of the children in the class. They appreciated the personal attention, and their work generally proceeded without the disruptions that were much more common in my early lessons.

The busy and productive hum of his classes was in marked contrast to the ragged questioning and comments that consistently disrupted student activities during my sessions. This provided me with a model of a more effective way of checking student progress and providing more effective feedback.

—E.S.

THINK: ASSESSING STUDENT PERFORMANCE OR BEHAVIOR

In a general sense teachers constantly monitor the progress of a lesson, asking "How are things going in this lesson?" As they observe student activities and behavior and talk with students about their work, therefore, they gain an understanding of how well the students understand the information or perform the required activities. Teachers also need to interpret the information gained, to assess each student's performance. They therefore engage in a process of reflection and analysis to understand the nature of the problems they are observing. As teachers observe students' activities, therefore, they will:

Analyze

- Identify problems, issues, gaps, or inadequacies in student work

- Establish reasons for these problems, for example, lack of understanding, carelessness, and so on.

- Identify key issues requiring an instructional process

Assess

- Evaluate the quality of each student's work

- Assess whether students understand the content of the work

- Assess whether students are clear about the activities they need to engage

---

PEDAGOGICAL WATCHFULNESS

In a recent class one of my students commented on the way I monitored my students. "I notice the way you watch us as we work. You really seem to keep an eye on us; to notice what we are doing. You always seem to have a comment to make at the right time. I really like the way you do that. You seem to understand what is happening to us as we work!"

   It reminds me of the wonderful words of Ted Aoki, who suggests the need for us to be more properly oriented to what teaching is: an attitude of pedagogical watchfulness and pedagogical thoughtfulness. "A watchfulness that is filled with the hope that wherever they may be the students do well and be well, and no harm will befall them," "hope for the well-being of the departing student..." (Pinar & Reynolds, 1992, p. 26).

—E.S.

ACT: AFFIRMING AND REMEDIATING

Teachers affirm student learning by providing positive feedback for good performance, and presenting advice that assists students to improve or extend their work. When teachers are clear on the nature of problems, their students experience they can succeed.

Reinforce Appropriate Performances or Behaviors

Let students know what they are doing right. Use that as a starting place to move to issues with which they are having difficulty. Provide comments that reinforce the positive aspects of their performance. Ask students what they think about their work.

Repeat Instructions

In some circumstances it is clear that students do not understand clearly the nature or steps in the activity in which they are engaged. Teachers may repeat their instructions, clarifying issues that seem problematic and sometimes providing more detailed guidance. Sometimes peers can assist here.

Demonstrate

Show students what to do. You can demonstrate a procedure, a process, or an activity so they know how it is done. This is especially important where skill development is required. Students should copy the process, but insert their own content. Merely copying a teacher-produced activity is a poor basis for learning.

Celebrate Success

Find ways of celebrating students' successful performance. Positive comments or some form of recognition encourages students. Children sharing their work to the class is another way to celebrate successful work.

CASE EXAMPLE 4.1: PUBLIC SPEAKING (II)— A DIRECT INSTRUCTION LESSON

The description of this lesson provides an example of the ways that the Look–Think–Act action research framework assisted the teacher to organize and monitor the ongoing teaching/learning activities in her classroom.

The description enables the reader to see how the teacher used the Look–Think–Act process to extend the lesson on persuasive speaking presented in the previous chapter.

As with previous examples, the Look–Think–Act elements are not always sequential. Teachers may cycle between Look and Think a number of times, for instance, before an "Act" is engaged. The important issue is to keep track of the different processes involved—whether students or teacher are acquiring information (Look), analyzing or sorting and selecting (Think), or engaging some activity (Act).

Subject: Language Arts

Grade: 7

Unit: Public Speaking

Topic: Persuasive Speech

Duration: Four 90-Minute Class Periods

New Jersey State Standards

3.2 *Writing:* D. Writing Forms, Audiences, and Purposes

3.3 *Speaking:* A. Discussion. B. Questioning and Contributing. C. Word Choice. D. Oral Presentation

Materials: Papers, pencils, pens, direction sheet (guidelines for delivering a persuasive speech), pocket dictionary, topics for a persuasive speech, video of speeches, speech handout

Accommodations/Modifications: One-on-one instruction if necessary, peer tutors, provide step-by-step instructions, have appropriate reading materials, check on progress regularly, have an aide and assistive technology if possible, work with a special educator to modify instruction

Bilingual English Language Learner Strategies: Peer tutors; labels in student(s)' language; word walls in native tongue and English; adapted texts; instructions and directions in representative/native language if possible; utilization of visuals such as pictorial schematics, graphic organizers, charts to illustrate concepts, directions, and so on

PHASE 1: PRESENTATION—Anticipatory Set

Objectives/ outcomes	Teacher instruction	Student learning	Assessment
Students will: Recall the elements of persuasion. Demonstrate understanding of persuasion by preparing a persuasive speech.	**Look** Teacher asks students to recall the effective elements of persuasion they learned in the previous class.	**Look** Students respond with effective elements of persuasion they learned previously.	Teacher will note extent of student understanding of elements of persuasive speech.
	Think Teacher asks students to identify elements in their own speeches by putting a star next to each element.	**Think** Students identify each element they find in own speeches.	
	Look Teacher asks students how speakers hold their attention during a speech.	**Act** Students mark each element with a star.	Students note understanding and clarity on a scoring guide.
	Act Teacher lists student-identified elements on board.		

PHASE 2: PRESENTATION—Input/Modeling, Checking, Practicing

Objectives/ outcomes	Teacher instruction	Student learning	Assessment
Students will: Define the elements of persuasive speaking.	**TEACHER INPUT** **Act** Teacher identifies and defines additional key elements of effective persuasive speaking and lists them on chalkboard.	**Look** Students note elements of persuasive speaking.	
Identify the elements of good speaking.	**Look** Teacher asks students to suggest a summary definition of each element. Teacher provides examples of key elements, utilizing video of persuasive presentations	**Think** Students suggest definitions for each element.	
	Think Teacher asks students to discuss how speakers hold an audience's attention— body language, articulation, pronunciation, pitch, speed, pauses and volume.	**Act** Students engage in discussion about what speakers do to hold an audience's attention.	
	MODELING **Act** Teacher presents a speech, accentuating the elements of effective persuasive speaking.	**Look** Students listen to speech.	
	CHECK FOR UNDERSTANDING **Think/Act** Teacher asks students questions about the elements of effective speaking, beginning with basic knowledge and advancing to critical thinking levels. Teacher reviews poorly understood concepts before engaging the class in a practice exercise.	**Think/Act** Students answer questions demonstrating their understanding of elements of effective speaking.	Teacher assesses levels of understanding of elements for each student. Responses to questions indicate level of

(Continued)

PHASE 2 (Continued)

Objectives/ outcomes	Teacher instruction	Student learning	Assessment
Students will: Demonstrate appropriate public speaking and listening skills—body language, articulation, pronunciation, pitch, speed, pauses, volume.	**GUIDED PRACTICE** **Act** Teacher instructs students to work in pairs to read their prepared speech to each other to check for clarity and understanding. Teacher circulates, listening and intervening when necessary to make comments and corrections.	**Act** Students practice their speeches with student partners.	understanding and need for clarification. Students check for clarity and understanding, using the scoring guide assigned previously.

PHASE 3: PRACTICE (Independent Practice): Review, Reflect, Construct/Perform

Objectives/ outcomes	Teacher instruction	Student learning	Assessment
Students will: Demonstrate appropriate public speaking and listening skills—body language, articulation, pronunciation, pitch, speed, pauses, volume.	**INDEPENDENT PRACTICE** **Act** Teacher instructs students to practice their speeches at home. She provides a framework of activities for this purpose.	**INDEPENDENT PRACTICE** Students practice speech at home, to prepare them for delivery in class. **Look** Review the speech script they have written. **Think** Note gaps or errors and modify the script.	

Objectives/ outcomes	Teacher instruction	Student learning	Assessment
		Act Present speech to members of their family or friends. **Look/Think** Discuss the effectiveness of the speech with their audience, taking particular note of the elements of good persuasive speech. **Act** Repeat the performance until the speech is performed effectively.	
	PERFORMANCE **Look/Think** Teacher observes and assesses student performances.	**PERFORMANCE** **Act** Each student presents his/her speech to the class.	Teacher and students assess adequacy of graphic organizer, script, and speech, identifying strengths and weaknesses, errors, or deficiencies. Teacher provides a written assessment and commentary on each student's work.

CONCLUSION

The apparently simple task of instruction masks a more complex process of education that provides teachers with the challenging task of dealing with a multitude of issues in order to accomplish effective student learning. As this chapter suggests, the busy hum of a productive classroom can only be accomplished by taking into account all of the factors that come to bear on a student's progress through schooling. Teachers need to take into account the natural capacities of their children, the body of knowledge and skills they acquire in the course of their early family and community experience, and the extensive body of knowledge that is incorporated into any school curriculum. Action research, as a process of inquiry, assists teachers to keep track of this array of issues so they are able to provide interesting and exciting lessons that engage their students and enable them to accomplish learning to the full extent of their capabilities. The following lesson provides an example of the way this happens, using continuing cycles of Look–Think–Act to monitor the progress of students through the activities and events comprising a persuasive teaching lesson.

LEARNING RESOURCES

Reflection

1. **Look**: Review the conditions of learning in this chapter.

   Think: Identify the main issues that affect children's learning.

   Act: Discuss these issues with a partner or some partners, and list how this information influences lesson planning.

2. **Look**: Review the domains of knowledge presented in this chapter.

   Think: Identify the different types of activities required for students to learn knowledge or skills in each domain.

   Act: Discuss and record with a partner or some partners the way that this information should be included in lesson planning.

3. **Look**: Review the Look–Think–Act cycle for reviewing student learning.

   Think: Identify the main ways that teachers can monitor student learning.

   Act: Discuss and record with partners the actions needed to (a) assess student performances and (b) identify and remediate weaknesses.

Web Sites

Review on Effective Instructional Methods From Educational and Psychological Research:

http://findarticles.com/p/articles/mi_m0FCG/is_1_32/ai_n13670698

The site offers a review of effective instructional methods from educational and psychological research.

Empowering New Teachers: Bank Street College of Education:

www.edutopia.org/bank-street-video

The Bank Street College provides aspiring educators new and innovative practice, with a focus on experiential learning, classroom immersion, and mentoring.

Monitoring Student Learning in the Classroom:

www.nwrel.org/scpd/sirs/2/cu4.html

This site identifies the practice of monitoring student learning as an essential component of high-quality education.

Understanding Student Learning:
www.iml.uts.edu.au/learnteach/enhance/understand
   This site explores the distinction between deep approaches and surface approaches to learning.

Additional Reading

Brooks, J., & Brooks, M. (2000). *In search of understanding: The case for constructivist classrooms* (2nd ed.). Upper Saddle River, NJ: Prentice Hall.

Cruikshank, D. (2006). *The act of teaching*. New York: McGraw-Hill.

Falk, B., & Blumenreich, M. (2005). *The power of questions: A guide to teacher and student research*. Portsmouth, NH: Heinemann.

Gardner, H. (2006). *Changing minds: The art and science of changing our and other people's minds*. Boston: Harvard Business School.

Joyce, B., Weil, M., & Calhoun, E. (2005). *Models of teaching: MyLabSchool* (7th ed.). Boston: Allyn & Bacon.

Silver, H., Strong, R., & Perini, M. (2000). *So each may learn: Integrating learning styles and multiple intelligences*. Alexandria, VA: ASCD.

NOTE

1. We are indebted to Rabbi Chaim Feuerman, professor of education at Yeshiva University New York, for his assistance in developing the Index of Engagement.

Action Learning

Accomplishing Objectives, Outcomes, and Standards

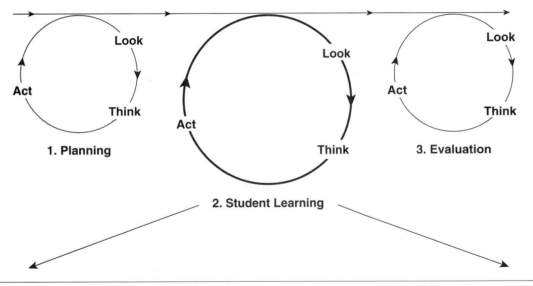

Instruction Phase: Parallel Process—Student Learning

This chapter describes how action learning, like action research, provides a useful framework to assist in organizing and keeping track of student learning.

It first focuses on the natural curiosity that makes children such efficient learners. This spirit of inquiry is harnessed by *action learning,* a process of learning in which students:

- **Look:** *Focusing* on an issue or topic, and *gathering information* from interviews, observations, surveys, books, records, videos, and media

- **Think:** Processing that information—*analyzing* by reviewing information and selecting key elements, and *synthesizing* by organizing into *categories and themes*

- **Act:** *Using* or *applying* the outcomes of that investigation in reports, *presentations,* and *performances*

Within this framework the chapter then presents:

- Potential sources of information

- Strategies for gathering and recording information (Look)

- Processes for analysis and synthesis of information (Think)

- Methods for preparing reports and presentations, and applying the outcomes of inquiry (Act)

ACTION LEARNING: STUDENT PROCESSES OF INQUIRY

The two previous chapters focused on elements of instruction—lesson planning and instruction. As we indicated in Chapter 1, however, the processes of planning and instruction are directly related to student learning. Teacher action research processes have a parallel process that engages students in actively participating in the construction of and reflection on their own learning (see Figure 5.1). As teachers Look, Think, and Act on their instructional strategies, they assist students to Look, Think, and Act on their learning, a process we call *action learning.*

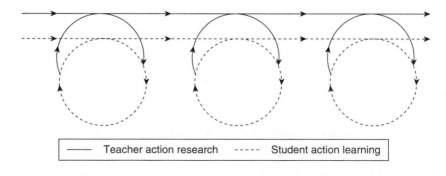

| —— Teacher action research   ----- Student action learning |

Figure 5.1   Teacher Action Research and Student Action Learning

This chapter therefore describes the ways teachers can assist students in the process of consciously constructing and reflecting on their learning. By these means we not only provide powerful and effective learning processes, but also enable students to acquire the skills through which they become lifelong learners.

CHILDREN AND LEARNING

Children are natural and extremely efficient learners. In the first years of their lives, they acquire a vast network of knowledge and skills that enable them to navigate the complex and difficult tasks required of human social life. They master the language that enables them to communicate with others, develop motor skills that provide the means for them to become mobile and physically self-sufficient, and acquire the cognitive and intellectual skills that enable them to "make sense" of their environment, and build a complex body of knowledge that allows them to navigate the complex interactions of social life. They have an incredible capacity to copy the behaviors and acts of those around them, and to participate easily in the complex rituals involved in even the apparently most simple of social events—eating a meal, getting dressed, asking a question, and so on.

Small children are naturally curious and will sometimes spend long periods playing with a small twig or a piece of string. As the following narrative demonstrates, what we call "play" is, in fact, children at work, investigating and testing out their environment, learning by investigating and testing the information and skills they need to live in their family and community. Children are the world's ultimate action learners.

PLAY: THE CHILD AT WORK

I recently watched two 3-year-olds playing around a puddle in a park in my community. I couldn't see what was so intriguing—a small frog, insect, or other creature—but they constantly circled the puddle, chattering animatedly with each other about what they were seeing, jumping back gleefully when it moved, following its path through the puddle. I was transfixed by their playful curiosity and the intensity of their exploration of this tiny part of their world. Long after I tired of watching them, and as I strolled away I could, as I looked back, see them continuing their journey of playful discovery, their laughter and liveliness bringing a smile of quiet joy to my face. As an educator I was forcefully reminded how, given the right circumstances and conditions, children are wonderfully engaged learners, and know our task as teachers is to unleash the beautiful potential of the inquisitive child. We don't need to make the child learn; we need merely to provide them with the right conditions that whets their natural appetite for new knowledge, and let them loose!

—E.S.

Learning as a process of inquiry, exploration, or investigation therefore is based on the assumption that children have a natural capacity to learn, and that our task is not to merely provide a body of knowledge, but to ask questions or provide other stimuli that will set their minds working and engage them in active and playful processes of discovery. It is this assumption that drives the techniques and processes described in this book. The underlying task of teaching is to engage children with the world in which they live, seek the questions that will arouse their curiosity, and provide the materials or context that will enable them to explore the issue or phenomenon that captures their attention. When we successfully accomplish these tasks, children become interested and excited learners, and teaching becomes a task of facilitating and extending the learning that is taking place. Children are natural action learners. Our task is merely to provide the context and extend and refine their investigative skills.

Action learning therefore provides an orientation to instruction that enables students to systematically investigate issues arising in their classroom, family, and community life. Centrally, it also provides the means by which students can learn ways of acquiring knowledge that greatly strengthens their ability to deal with the complexities of life in the modern world. By providing them with the tools of systematic inquiry and investigation, teachers enable their students to become lifelong learners, able to investigate issues and problems rigorously and to acquire strongly based and substantiated knowledge. It enables them to become independent and practiced thinkers, to analyze issues clearly, and to gain greater understanding about the complex issues they will confront in their everyday lives. As the following narrative demonstrates, even the academically less talented have the capacity to use action learning processes to demonstrate highly complex learning that can greatly enrich their lives and increase their self-esteem.

AN ENGAGED ACTION LEARNER

As a young teacher I gave my Grade 6 students the opportunity to construct a social studies project of their own choice. After a week's work, including time in class, but also work at home, my students presented their projects to their assigned group. The project voted "best" by the group was then presented to the whole class.

I still have vivid memories of Bill's project on the Antarctic. Bill was not a good student. He struggled with his work on a daily basis, his academic gifts were limited, and his grades were always marginal at best. As his teacher I provided the best assistance and support I could, and met with his mother fairly regularly to find ways to boost his achievement. Personally, however, he was a "plodder," and it was difficult to engage his attention, or to motivate him to produce anything other than the least he could get away with.

It was with some surprise, then, that when, in response to my question "Whose project has been chosen from this group?" Bill rose proudly from his seat and walked to the front of the class. For the next

10 minutes the children sat transfixed as Bill presented them with a detailed and highly informative account of the nature of the frozen continent and the life within and around it. He told of icebergs—different from those of the Arctic because they were flat and not jagged; of the depth of snow that covered the interior; of human exploration of the continent; of the scientific bases there, the scientists that manned them, and their scientific work. He told of the teeming life within the ocean and the whaling that had decimated the whale populations; the changing seasons; and the dangers of early exploration, providing vivid accounts of sailing ships locked in the ice and the struggle of sailors to sail back to land in open boats.

As he talked, the class transfixed by his narrative, he provided vivid illustrations that were assembled in his large project book and complemented by books loaned from the local library. Careful illustrations provided additional sources of information, and each photograph or illustration was accompanied by carefully scripted notes that described or explained its significance.

This memory still makes my heart beat a little faster, reminds me of why I am a teacher and of the human potential that is at the heart of *all* of our students. It prompts me to stay in touch with the possibilities for each of the teachers in my charge, and takes me to the heart of my profession. Thank you, Bill, for that wonderful memory.

—E.S.

ACTION LEARNING: PROCESSES OF INQUIRY AND INVESTIGATION

Like action research, action learning is a process of inquiry or investigation that leads to the acquisition of new knowledge and skills. As with action research, students acquire and analyze information, and make use of the knowledge they have generated. The following sections provide a more detailed description of how steps in an action learning cycle (see Figure 5.2) can assist students to achieve the learning outcomes incorporated into school curricula and embodied in state standards. The processes of action learning include:

- **Look:** Clarifying the topic to be explored and gathering relevant information
- **Think:** Processing the information—reflecting, analyzing, and synthesizing
- **Act:** Using or applying the outcomes of that investigation

LOOK: FOCUSING AND GATHERING INFORMATION

This first step of an action research cycle focuses on gathering and recording information. Although students will quite naturally start to process information as it is

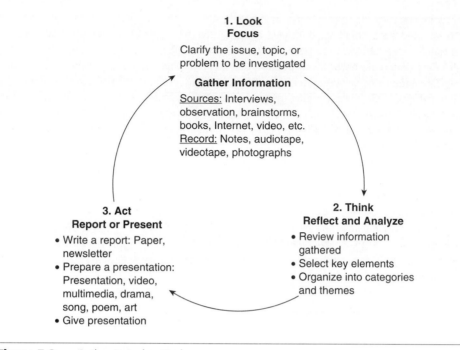

Figure 5.2   Action Learning Cycle

gathered, it is important to allow students to explore the wide range of sources available to them, recording interesting or relevant pieces of information as they go.

FOCUSING

Teachers need to stimulate the children's interest and excite them with the possibility of exploring a topic or issue. The teacher works with the students to determine the focus of their studies—a topic or issue to investigate, or a problem to solve. Topics may be very broad (a study of birds of America), or quite specific (the effect of protectionism on the U.S. economy). The nature of the topic will depend on the age, capacities, and interests of the students, and on the standards to be accomplished.

GATHERING INFORMATION

Teachers then assist students to identify sources and types of information relevant to the topic or issue to be studied.

Information Sources

Teachers help students to identify a variety of information sources and resources. These may include:

- Brainstorms:
  o Sharing information they already know

- Literature reviews:

  o Books in the library
  o Original sources
  o Newspapers
  o Documents

- Interviews with people who have relevant knowledge or experiences

- Observation:
  o Watching people perform activities
  o Events—festivals, city council meeting, and so on
  o Cultural settings—a zoo, a factory, city hall, the school yard, and so on
  o Demonstrations—By teachers, students, community members

- Surveys

- Listening:
  o Teacher presentation
  o Guest speakers
  o Field trips

- Web searches

- Photography

- Films and videos

Recording Information

As students explore these sources, they will need to record significant items of information for later use. They may record information in any of the following ways:

- Note taking:
  o Summarizing information contained in literature
  o Recording what people say in an interview
  o Taking notes that describe events, activities, demonstrations, field trips, and so on

- Audiotape recording of:
  - Interviews
  - Presentations

- Videotape recording of:
  - Presentations
  - Activities

- Observation schedule, recording particular features of an event or activity

- Questionnaires

- Photographs

Information may be recorded on tapes or disks, in notebooks, on charts, or with cameras.

PROCEDURES FOR INTERVIEWS, OBSERVATIONS, AND SURVEYS

Interviews

The purpose of an interview is to allow a person to present an account of activities or events in which they have participated, or that they have observed. Interviews are a particularly effective means of recording oral histories of the local community. The type of questions used are important, as they must stimulate the person to remember what occurred and enable them to describe events, activities, and settings in detail. It is important, however, that interview questions are open ended and quite broad to allow the respondent—the person interviewed—to describe events in his or her own terms. Interview questions may include:

Grand tour questions. A grand tour question has the general form, "Can you tell me about. . ." The grand tour question is very general, and can take a number of forms, for example:

- Can you tell me about the town where you were raised?
- Can you tell me about your trip to the White House?
- Can you tell me about your work?
- Can you tell me what happened the last time you . . . ? (And so on.)

Follow-up questions. Follow-up questions encourage a respondent to provide more details about issues or events they have raised. They take a number of forms:

- Can you tell me more about . . . ?

- What else happened?

- Can you give me an example of . . . ?

Guided tour questions. Students can ask a respondent to show them around a place where events occur—to take a "guided tour." As the respondent shows them around, they can ask guided tour and follow-up questions. As they are shown the setting, they can ask grand tour and follow-up questions:

- Can you tell me about this place?

- What else happens here? (And so on.)

Task-related questions. Students can ask a respondent to demonstrate an activity, describe how an activity is done, or draw a picture, diagram, or map. They can ask grand tour and follow-up questions as the demonstration or activity occurs:

- Can you tell me what you're doing?

- Can you tell me about that picture? (And so on.)

Extension questions. Who, What, How, Where, When, Why.
     After people have responded to grand tour or guided tour questions, students may seek more detailed information using the following forms of question:

- *Who* else comes to this community center?

- *What* do they do?

- *How* do they go about doing that?

- *When* do they do that?

- *Where* do they mainly do that?

- *Why* do they do that?

Preparing for an interview. Prior to an interview, students should prepare an interview schedule—a list of questions that will guide their interview (see Figure 5.3). They should think carefully about the purpose of the interview, the type of information they wish to acquire, and the main topic of the interview. They also need to think about how they will introduce themselves and when and where they will carry out the interview.

INTERVIEW SCHEDULE: TOWN HISTORY

Introduction

Hello! My name is Sarah Jones. I'm a student at Kennedy Middle School, and I'm studying the history of this town. My teacher, Mr. Jefferson, said that you have lived here for a long time and might be able to tell me what the town was like when you were growing up here. Would you be willing to talk to me about your experience of growing up in this town?

(When can I talk to you? Where can we talk? Do you mind if I take notes? Use a tape recorder?)

Grand Tour Question

Can you tell about your experience growing up in . . . ?

Follow-Up Questions

Can you tell me anything else about the town at that time?
What else happened?

Guided Tour Question

Could we go for a walk through the neighborhood where you were raised?

Task-Related Questions

Could you draw me a map of your neighborhood? The town?
Can you tell me about it?

Extension Questions

- *Who* else lived in your neighborhood?
- *What* were the main things you did (activities)?
- *What* are the main things that happened (events)?
- *How* did people respond to those activities/events?
- *When* did those things (activities/events) happen?
- *Where* did they mainly occur?
- *Why* did people do those things?

Conclusion

You've been most helpful. May I ask you to read my project when I write it up? I'd like to check that it is accurate.

I've enjoyed talking with you very much. Thank you for your time. Goodbye.

Figure 5.3 An Interview Schedule

Students should practice interviews in class, using the interview schedule they have prepared. They should check whether their questions are appropriate, and practice taking notes.

When they have completed a draft of their report, they should show it to their respondent to check its accuracy. As a courtesy they should also provide each respondent with a copy of the final report.

Observation

Preparing an observation schedule. Students may prepare an observation schedule to guide their observations of events or settings. The schedule assists them to focus on the many facets of an event or scene—the place or location, people involved, activities, actions, time and duration, and purposes. These are often presented as six questions— Where, Who, What, How, When, and Why (see Figure 5.4). Younger students may record their observations directly in the schedule, taking notes of their observations, but older students will need a notebook to record more extensive observations. Students should practice an observation using a schedule in class, or for homework.

OBSERVATION SCHEDULE

Event and Setting

The following notes relate to observations of a Harvest Festival at the Harvard Memorial Church in Livingstone.

Where is the church located?

Who is involved in the harvest festival?

What is happening? What are the main activities?

How are they carried out? What are people doing?

When do they occur?

Why are people doing these activities? What is the purpose?

Figure 5.4   An Observation Schedule

Surveys

Surveys are a useful way for students to obtain information about specific topics from a large group of people. Questionnaires that form the basis of a survey may be used to interview people (see Figure 5.5), or may be given to people to provide a written response to questions. Students should prepare a questionnaire and practice both forms of response—verbal and written. The following procedures assist students to construct a questionnaire:

Focus. What do you wish to discover? What is the main topic? Which people will you ask?

Instructions:

Provide clear instructions to respondents.

Tell them precisely how to complete the form or answer the questions.

Give examples, if possible.

Questions:

All issues or topics related to the main topic should be identified and framed as a question.

Each question should:

- Be clear, straightforward, and to the point

- Only contain one issue or topic

- Be framed in positive terms (e.g., "Girls should be allowed to wear short skirts to school," rather than "Girls should not be allowed to wear short skirts to school")

- Should only contain terms that can be understood by respondents

Responses:

Answers should be in appropriate format, depending on the information required:

- *Open response*—Students should have _____ minutes to leave the school after final class.

- *Fixed response*—How long should students have to leave the school after final class? 15 minutes _____ 20 minutes _____ 30 minutes _____ 40 minutes _____

- *Dual response*—Answers requiring one of two responses: Yes/No, True/False, Agree/Disagree. For example, Girls should be allowed to wear short skirts to school. Agree_____ Disagree _____

- *Rating response*—Questions requiring a scale of responses. For example, Strongly agree_____ Agree_____ Neutral _____ Disagree_____ Strongly Disagree _____

Students will also need to prepare a response sheet to tally the responses to each question. It may look like the one shown in Figure 5.6.

STUDENT QUESTIONNAIRE: SCHOOL CLOTHING

Hello! My name is Cynthia. My class is doing a survey about school clothing. Can I ask you a few questions? It will only take a few minutes and your answers will be kept confidential.

1. Do you think students at this school should have to wear a uniform?
   Yes _____ No _____

2. Are you happy with the current school clothing policy? Yes _____ No _____

3. When should students be able to stop wearing a school uniform? Year 8 _____ Year 9 _____
   Year 10 _____ Year 11 _____ Year 12 _____

4. Who should decide whether a student is wearing appropriate clothing? Principal and Deputy Principals _____ Teachers _____ Parents _____ Students _____

5. Could you say how strongly you agree or disagree with the following statement?
   "The current school clothing policy is too restrictive."
   Strongly Agree _____ Agree _____ No Opinion _____ Disagree _____ Strongly Disagree _____

6. What would you do to improve the school clothing policy?

Thank you for your time. We will provide a report on our survey in the next school newsletter.

Figure 5.5   A Survey Questionnaire

**SCHOOL CLOTHING SURVEY:
RESPONSE SHEET**

1. Do you think students at this school should have to wear a uniform?

   YES ....Total ....
   NO ....Total ....

2. Are you happy with the current school clothing policy?

   YES ....Total ....
   NO ....Total ....

3. When should students be able to stop wearing a school uniform?

   Year 8 .... Total ....
   Year 9 .... Total ....
   Year 10 ....Total ....
   Year 11 ....Total ....
   Year 12 ....Total ....

4. Who should determine whether a student is wearing appropriate clothing?

   Principal and Deputy Principals ....Total ....
   Teachers ....Total ....
   Parents ....Total ....
   Students ....Total ....

5. Could you say how strongly you agree or disagree with the following statement?

   "The current school clothing policy is too restrictive."
   Strongly Agree ....Total ....
   Agree ....Total ....
   No Opinion ....Total ....
   Disagree ....Total ....
   Strongly Disagree ....Total ....

6. What would you do to improve the school clothing policy?

   ....
   ....
   ....
   ....
   ....
   ....
   ....

[Place a check mark beside each response and add the totals for each response.

For question 6, summarize the major responses. Place a check mark next to any responses that are similar, and record the total for each.]

Figure 5.6   Survey Response Sheet

THINK: REFLECTION AND ANALYSIS

In the previous section students used a range of techniques to gather information by talking, looking, listening, smelling, and touching. In the process they obtained many discrete pieces of information related to the topic or issue they investigated. The next step is to review that information and subject it to analysis so that they can "make sense" of it. From the large body of information they have collected, they select the key elements or features that are central to an understanding of the issue or topic and organize it into a coherent set of topics and subtopics.

This process mirrors features within the comprehension, analysis, and synthesis categories of the Bloom Taxonomy. Students process the information they have acquired to grasp its meaning, break it down into component parts, make sense of it, organize it (analysis), and combine selected elements to produce a new or original account or understanding (synthesis). These key elements or features provide the basis for writing a report or project or giving a presentation. We might see this process as similar to drawing a picture, or doing a jigsaw puzzle, so that by analyzing and synthesizing information, students are assembling the materials from which they will build a word picture.

This is a very creative task but one that can be quite demanding, as there are no fixed rules or "correct" answers to the process of selecting, sorting, and organizing information, just as there is no correct way to draw a picture. Younger children may require rubrics or frameworks that assist them in the task and enable them to grasp the fundamentals of data analysis.

As they engage in the process of analysis, students should think of the *purpose* for doing so. Analysis provides the material for writing a report or preparing a presentation, so they should keep this in mind as they work. They should ask themselves, "For whom am I/are we writing the report?" "What will that audience find interesting or significant?" "What should I/we tell them that will enable them to understand the most interesting and important things about this topic or issue?"

ANALYSIS: SELECTING IMPORTANT, SIGNIFICANT, OR INTERESTING PIECES OF INFORMATION[1]

The task of analysis requires students to:

- Review information
- Select key elements or themes
- Identify related pieces of information for each key element or theme

Students may ask themselves (or the teacher may ask):

- Of all the information I/you have gathered, what are the most important pieces—what are the key things I/you have learned about this topic or issue?

- What can I/you say about each of these key pieces of information? What details about the key piece do I have in the information I have collected?

If children are reading books and other materials, they need to select the most important or significant pieces of information, and then identify related pieces of information that extend their understanding of the topic—that enable them to "build a picture" of that topic.

If they are watching events that occur in a social setting, they may use a simple framework of questions to assist them in the process of selecting key pieces of information:

- *What* are the most important things (acts, activities) happening here?

- *Who* is involved?

- *How* do the people go about doing the acts and activities? Who is doing what?

- *Why* are they doing what they are doing? What is the purpose of the activity?

- *Where* do these acts and activities occur?

- *When* did these activities happen? In what order (the sequence of events)?

As they review their body of "data" (information), they therefore select key elements or themes, and then identify related pieces of information that will enable them to provide significant or interesting details about that theme.

SYNTHESIS: ORGANIZING A SYSTEM OF CATEGORIES[2]

Once key elements and features of a topic have been identified, they are then sorted into logical sets of categories and subcategories. Students may identify the key features of the event as major themes, and then decide which categories (and their associated subcategories) should be included in each theme. The organized system of themes, categories, and subcategories then provides the outline for a report.

Figure 5.7 presents a system of categories for the topic "Visiting the Zoo," which includes categories made up of the original elements identified in student analysis:

- Themes included "Traveling to the zoo," "The animals and birds," "What the children did," and so on.

TOPIC: VISITING THE ZOO

Traveling to the zoo

- Getting on the bus
- Driving through town
- Arriving at the zoo

The animals and birds

- Cages
- Enclosures
- Animals: Monkeys, elephants, hippopotamuses, snakes, zebras, bears, tigers
- Birds: Cassowary, parrots, cranes, ibis, hawks
- Activity: Playing, sleeping, flying, standing
- Feeding time

What the children did

- Watching: Keeping a safe distance, naughty boys
- Talking: Whispering, yelling, arguing
- Playing: Running around, ignoring the teacher

What teachers and parents did

- Took us around
- Described the animals
- Yelled at the naughty boys

What I learned

- A snake may only eat occasionally.
- Tigers are cats.
- Monkeys can be mischievous.
- We need to enjoy and respect all forms of life on this planet.

Figure 5.7   A System of Categories

- Categories within "The animals and birds" theme included "Cages, Enclosures, Animals, Birds, Activity, and Feeding time."

- Elements of "Animals" included "monkeys, elephants, hippopotamuses, snakes, zebras, bears, tigers."

The process of analysis and synthesis therefore involves:

- Reviewing information

- Selecting the major themes, or key elements (categories)

- Identifying related pieces of information (elements)

- Organizing and listing them in ways that will provide the basis for a report

The final product is a framework of categories that provides the headings, sub-headings, and topics for a report (see the next section).

ACT: REPORTING, PRESENTING, AND PERFORMING

In this third step of the Look–Think–Act process, students use the outcomes of their analysis, reporting on the topic or issue they have investigated, or using the information they have gathered. This is the "Application" section of Bloom's Taxonomy, in which students prepare, produce, report, relate, show, or use the information they have acquired in new and concrete ways. This is an exciting part of the process, as students get to see the outcomes of their research as they construct creative reports, presentations, and performances that enhance their learning and provide life and vitality to their classrooms (see Figure 5.8, and Powerful Presentations and Performances on p. 112).

Written reports are common, but more creative projects may incorporate:

- Illustrations

- Photographs

- Graphs

- Art

- Maps

They may be presented in many forms of written report:

- Papers

- Booklets

- Newspapers

- Journals

- Newsletters

- Brochures

- Posters

- Collages

- Mosaics

- Advertisements

In this electronic age students can also construct:

- Multimedia presentations

- Videos

- Wikis

- Blogs

Any of these presentations may incorporate:

- Poems

- Songs

- Music

- Drama—plays, role plays, simulations, skits, and so on

- Dance

- Visual art

These exciting possibilities not only enable students to learn and demonstrate new skills, but provide the context for profound learning experiences that touch their lives in significant ways. In these ways, students demonstrate their competence, show how they have attained state standards, and provide the means for teachers to move toward student assessments that are not only rigorous, but more clearly attuned to the realities of everyday life. Students demonstrate deeper levels of understanding by embedding discrete pieces of knowledge in artifacts that comprise the context of their everyday lives.

STUDENT REPORTS, PRESENTATIONS, AND PERFORMANCES		
Advertisements	Hats	Radio shows
Bingo games	Interactive bulletin boards	Recordings
Board games	Interviews	Relief maps
Books and booklets	Journals	Research
Book reviews	Letters	Riddles
Brochures	Magazines	Role plays
Building from boxes	Matching games	Scrapbooks
Bulletin boards	Mime skits	Service projects
Cartoons	Mobiles	Simulations
Center activities	Mock news broadcasts	Slide productions
Charts	Models and prototypes	Sociodrama
Choral readings	Murals	Speakers
Clay depictions	Music	Storytelling
Collages	Newspapers	Surveys
Collections	Newsletters	Tape recordings
Computer games	Paintings	Telegrams
Cooking activities	Pamphlets	Transparencies
Crossword puzzles	Podcasts	Trips
Dance	Posters	Television shows
Designs	Panels	Twenty questions
Diaries	Panoramas	Testimonials
Digital photographs	Pen pals	Travel itineraries
Dioramas	Period pieces	Variety shows
Exhibits	Photographs	Video productions
Experiments	Plays	Verse
Films/filmstrips	Poems	Wikis
Flannel board games & stories	Political cartoons	World Wide Web pages
Flow charts	Postcards	Woodworking
Graphs	PowerPoint presentations	Yearbook writing
Guest speakers	Primary documents	Zenith—the sky is the limit
Hall of fame	Puzzles	—L.M.
Hanger art	Questionnaires	

Figure 5.8   Reports, Presentations, and Activities

OUTLINES AND SCRIPTS

The outcome of Steps 1 and 2 (Look and Think) of the action learning cycle was a framework of concepts and topics that provides the basis for formulating reports and presentations. The key themes and categories provide the main headings and subheadings of a report, and the elements provide the information to be included in each. Using the example "A Trip to the Zoo," the themes "Traveling to the zoo," "The animals and birds," "What the children did," and so on, would be used as the main headings. The category "Traveling to the zoo" would include subheadings "Getting on the bus," "Driving through town," and "Arriving at the zoo." Other headings and subheadings would be treated in similar fashion. Each of the elements within the subcategory becomes a topic from which sentences are constructed—for example, Getting on the bus: "The class lined up outside the school and then got excitedly on the bus when Mrs. Schroeder told them."

If students wish to present the outcomes of their research artistically or electronically, the framework of concepts and topics also provides the basis for developing a script.

Developing a Script

1. Identify audience (who will see our performance) and purpose (what we want them to know, understand).

2. Identify the main players (whose stories, activities we need to present).

3. From the data, identify information about each of those people we wish to include in the script.

4. Write a script that tells how people engage in the activities that are part of the story.

5. Review and edit the script.

6. Rehearse the performance.

POWERFUL PRESENTATIONS AND PERFORMANCES

I have seen some extraordinarily powerful presentations produced by students at all levels of the school. In my primary school classes, students wrote and produced plays, and then entertained other classes at the end of each term by taking their "troupe" from class to class around the school. Both players and performers gained a great deal of enjoyment from the process, and as a teacher I could see that it was educationally well grounded. In the process of writing, production, and performance, my students acquired a broad range of skills, honing them to high levels of accomplishment in order to be able to perform publicly. The joy and excitement of their learning was clearly evident in their purposefulness and in the liveliness that shone from their faces.

Since then I've seen many other performances, some of them quite stunning and deeply meaningful, emerge from action research projects carried out by students in classrooms and schools. A small sample includes:

1. A project engaged by children and teachers in a kindergarten class that recorded the way they developed a solution to the problem of local dogs who had begun straying into the school. Fearful that people would lose their pets to the dog catcher, the children discussed the situation, met with a vet, molded dogs from clay, counted the dogs around the school, and learned how people could care for their pets by reading books from the school library. They shared this knowledge by creating posters telling grown-ups how they could care for their dogs, and posted them at the local grocery store and at other places around town. Their campaign was successful in getting local people to make sure their dogs did not stray onto the school grounds. It thus also reduced the fear in children that dogs would be taken to the pound and destroyed.

2. High school students in a special education class for the learning impaired were disturbed to hear that funds for their work-study program were to be cut. They wrote scripts that described their work-study experiences and the benefit they attained from them. With support from their parents and teachers, they presented their report to the local education authorities and were successful in having funds returned to their program.

3. As members of a Student Action Committee, a group of students met several mornings before classes commenced to learn how to study their school and homes. The outcome of these studies was their recognition of the cultural diversity of their own community, and the need to raise student awareness of that diversity. As a result of their efforts, a course—American Cultural Studies—became part of the program of studies offered by their school.

4. A group of middle school girls met to discuss issues of sexual harassment that were affecting their school lives. As a result of a series of meetings, they decided to include some boys in their group and discovered that boys also suffered harassment. They formed a group called Students Against Harassment, and with the help of one of the teachers, wrote an article for the school newspaper, and produced a play called *Speaking Out* that depicted the effects of harassment on both girls and boys. They also produced a triptych, a three-paneled poster, where students could speak out about harassment by writing down their ideas after the performance. Their

performance was wildly applauded when presented at a student forum in the school, and the play went on to win a prize in a state student drama contest. Their efforts also had a practical outcome in that complaints of sexual harassment in the school decreased dramatically.

5. A teacher taught her students to use video cameras, and then had them record aspects of their home and community lives. The resulting documentary provided a powerful picture of the lives of students in this poor Hispanic community.

6. An expensive campaign to decrease smoking in a small city was largely unsuccessful. In evaluating the effects of the various parts of the campaign, the director of the project concluded that the most effective activity was a video documentary produced by a group of high school students. Researching the effects of smoking, the way that young people were drawn into smoking, and the impact of smoking on their health and well-being, the students wrote and produced a dramatic documentary that received wide coverage, not only in their city, but across their state and nationally.

—E.S.

CASE EXAMPLE 5.1: CIVIL RIGHTS

This lesson by a third-grade teacher demonstrates the diverse activities that can be used to facilitate student learning. The Look–Think–Act sequence assists the teacher to track the progress of the lesson, focusing separately on activities through which students acquire information, analyze or process that information, and engage in an action to either use it or demonstrate what they have learned.

Primary source documents helped children to **LOOK** and make observations; **THINK**, reflect, and interpret; and **ACT** to promote further inquiry. Photographs from the Web sites contained historical records that students used for their research. Newspaper articles from the era were also used. Dr. King's letter from the Birmingham jail was employed as a primary source document. Music from the movement was utilized as well, not only as primary source documents, but as new music for students to learn to sing.

A guest speaker, photographs, videos, literature, and interviews were all salient instructional strategies to assist young social studies learners to construct knowledge and learn about social justice. Initially, children **LOOKED** at literature that sparked their curiosity and energized their **THINKING**. Text illustrations and photographs also prompted questions and further exploration. Living vicariously through multiple multimedia sources prompted discussion about unfairness, discrimination, and prejudice from the third graders and moved them to **ACT**.

Topic: Voting Rights

Subjects: Literacy, Social Studies, Mathematics

Grade: Grade 3

Duration: 2–3 weeks

Alabama State Standards

Literacy

C 5. Interpret passages in print material; identifying main idea; drawing conclusions; determining cause and effect; identifying fact and opinion; summarizing passages; identifying author's purpose.

C 9. Use a wide range of strategies to interpret, evaluate, appreciate, and construct meaning from print materials; use a wide range of strategies to interpret, evaluate, appreciate, and construct meaning from print materials.

Social Studies

2. Describe physical characteristics, including landforms, bodies of water, soil, and vegetation of various places on earth.

8. Identify geographic links of land regions, river systems, and interstate highways.

11. Identify significant historical sites in Alabama, including locations of civil rights activities.

Mathematics

Demonstrate number sense by comparing, ordering, and expanding whole numbers through 9999.

Materials

Photos from PBS Kids' site: It's Not Fair: http://pbskids.org/wayback/fair/fighters/index.html

Give each group a photo and story from this PBS Kids' site:
http://pbskids.org/wayback/fair/pix/index.html
Poem about child labor
Students' reading/writing journals

Special Needs, Accommodations, and Modifications: One-on-one instruction if necessary, peer tutors, provide step-by-step instructions, have appropriate reading materials, check on progress regularly, have an aide and assistive technology if possible, work with a special educator to modify instruction

Bilingual English Language Learner Strategies: Peer tutors, labels in student(s)' language, word walls in native tongue and English, adapted texts, instructions and directions in representative/native language if possible, utilization of visuals such as pictorial schematics, graphic organizers, charts to illustrate concepts, directions, and so on

PHASE 1: EXPLORATION

Objectives/ outcomes	Teacher instruction	Student learning	Assessment
The students will develop observations and generalizations about inequality.	**Look** Ask students to view child labor photographs from a Web site. Ask students to read a poem about child labor. **Think** Ask students to discuss the inequality of what they observed, interpreted, and read. Ask them to make observations about what it must have been like working and living in the location and time where the photo was taken. **Act** Have students meet Mary Harris Jones at: http://pbskids.org/wayback/fair/fighters/fighters_05_2.html and read about her work to pass laws against child labor. Ask students to write in their journals as if they were a child in the early 1900s. They should say why they think that it is unfair to be a child working in a mill instead of in school.	**Look** In small groups students will examine child labor photographs. They will read poems about child labor in their groups. **Think** Students observe the Web site or photographs about child labor and discuss their reactions in their group. They describe what it must have been like by reading and examining the information given to them from the PBS Kids' site. **Act** Students meet Mary Harris Jones and learn of her work. Students engage in discussion about unfairness and danger of child labor. Students will select a child, gather information from the Web site, and write in their journal.	Reactions, observations, and generalizations about feelings of inequality written in the students' reading and writing journals depicting themselves as a particular child laborer from the early 1900s from photographs and poems.

PHASE 2: DEVELOPMENT

Materials

Chart paper

Littlesugar, A. (2001). *Freedom school, yes!* New York: Philomel.

Morrison, T. (2004). *Remember: The journey to school integration.* New York: Houghton Mifflin.

Jim Crow literacy tests

Photographs from the civil rights movement (be sure not to use photos that are too violent with young learners)

Be sure to use photos in which children were a part of the movement.

Remember has terrific photos.

Selma, Lord, Selma©—video

PBS Kids' Way Back site: http://pbskids.org/wayback/civilrights/features_school.html

http://pbskids.org/wayback/civilrights/snapshot.html

Maps

A Jim Crow literacy test

Objectives/ outcomes	Teacher instruction	Student learning	Assessment
Students will: Revise their generalizations by using a wide range of strategies to interpret, evaluate, appreciate, and construct meaning from print materials.	**Look** Lead a discussion about inequality. The teacher documents what is shared on chart paper.	**Look** The students discuss inequality and share what they wrote in their journals.	Revised generalizations through study of literacy tests
Use knowledge of letter–sound correspondence and structural analysis.	**Think** The teacher asks about other times in our nation's history when inequality was a problem.	**Think** The students think about times in history when they know that inequality and unfairness was a problem.	Narratives written by students about the visitors that lived through the civil rights movement or voting rights in Selma/Birmingham
Apply prior knowledge and experiences. Use knowledge of word meaning. Apply knowledge of sentence structure and context.	**Act** Ask students to share their views about inequalities, and what they know about people who led movements about fairness and equality. Ask students if they know about the march from Selma, Alabama, to Montgomery.	**Act** Students share what they know.	Digital photos and accompanying narratives, compilation of narratives to create a Journal and Class book about what they have learned so far
Preview and predict. Locate information in reference sources.	**Look** Show the videos *Bloody Sunday* and *Selma, Lord, Selma.*	**Look** Students view the video *Selma, Lord, Selma.*	

Objectives/ outcomes	Teacher instruction	Student learning	Assessment
Use a wide range of strategies to interpret, evaluate, appreciate, and construct meaning from print materials—fiction, nonfiction, poetry. *Social Studies* **Students will:** Describe physical characteristics, including landforms, bodies of water, soil, and vegetation of various places on earth. Identify geographic links of land regions, river systems, and interstate highways. Compare laws that pertain to citizens of the United States. Describe cultural, political, and economic characteristics of people in the Western Hemisphere. Describe functions of political units such as cities, states, and nations. Identify significant historical sites.	**Think** Ask students to write questions in their journals as they view videos. Read different types of children's literature about civil rights and discuss with children. **Act** Use primary document photos in *Remember* to prompt discussion. **Look** Ask students to observe the children included in many of the situations. Use photos and primary documents. **Think** Have students discuss their responses to photos of the behavior of police. **Act** In small groups, have students examine the text of Dr. Martin Luther King Jr.'s letter from the Birmingham Jail. Ask students to document what they determine as pertinent in their journals.	**Think** As they view videos students write questions in their journals. Students listen to children's literature about the 1960s and the civil rights movement. **Act** From the examination of the photos, students write reflections in their reading journals. **Look** Students will observe and discuss how children were a part of the struggle for equality and voting rights. **Think** Children describe their responses to the photos. **Act** Students read the letter from the Birmingham jail. Students document what they learn in their journals.	

(Continued)

PHASE 2 (Continued)

Objectives/ outcomes	Teacher instruction	Student learning	Assessment
	Have students fill out and then discuss the literacy tests that African Americans (during Jim Crow) had to fill out to register to vote. Use different Web sites to reinforce some of what students learn. The PBS TeacherSource Web Site is www.teachersdomain .org/35/soc/ush/civil/webb/	Students fill out "Literacy Tests," discuss, and write in their journals. **Look** Have students listen and watch Sheyann Webb talk about how she participated in the voting rights struggle as a 9-year-old. **Think** Have students discuss the Web cast about her reflection and compare it to the video of *Selma, Lord, Selma*.	
	Invite guest speakers in to speak about their encounters with civil rights events and issues. Ask students to make a list of questions for the visitor and take digital photos of guest speaker.	In pairs/groups, students will list interview questions to ask invited guests. Students listen to the guest speaker(s) invited from the civil rights movement. **Act**	
	Ask students to write up narratives about the guest speaker(s)' visit, illustrate their work, and use digital photos to create a class book about voting rights in Selma and Birmingham, Alabama.	Students take digital photos. They listen, ask interview questions, and document responses. Students work in groups to gather data, write up narratives, illustrate them, and create a voting rights book.	

PHASE 3: EXPANSION

Materials			
Web site: www.birminghampledge.org/ Chart paper, journals, sentence strips			

Objectives/ outcomes	Teacher instruction	Student learning	Assessment
Students will: Apply generalizations and observations about civil rights by developing a class plan about how to be respectful citizens. They will sign "The Birmingham Pledge," but first decide whether or not to.	**Look** Access The Birmingham Pledge at: www.birminghampledge.org/ and make copies for each student. **Think** Place students in small groups and ask them to discuss whether or not their group would sign the pledge. **Look** Ask students to reexamine The Birmingham Pledge and think about how to use this pledge to write a class pledge. **Think** Ask students to write a pledge that would make their classroom a more accepting environment where all classmates feel accepted. The teacher helps students think through some of these points, and writes their ideas on whiteboard or chart paper. **Act** Assist students to work together to gain consensus about their class pledge. Write the pledge on chart paper and display it.	**Look** Students read, reflect, and discuss the pledge. **Think** Students discuss whether they would sign the pledge or not. **Look** Students reexamine the pledge in groups to determine how they could use this as a model for a class pledge. **Think** Students work in groups to write sentence strips for a class pledge. **Act** Students work together to create a pledge.	Pledges found at: www.birminghampledge.org/signit/ The class plan applies students' generalizations about becoming respectful citizens. Sentences written in groups (on sentence strips). Chart paper with dictated ideas. Students' written pledges on chart paper.

Conclusion

Given the right environment, children are active and enthusiastic learners, capable of acquiring a broad range of knowledge and skills and producing sometimes remarkable outcomes from their efforts. The teacher's task is to provide the stimulus that lets loose this wonderful capability and provides the means for their students to engage in interesting and creative activities that not only extend their learning, but excite their imagination. The repetitive routines that are an integral part of any learning environment can gain richness and vitality by complementing them with the active learning methods presented above. Systematically framing learning processes as processes of inquiry, and using diverse strategies that assist students to acquire, analyze, and apply knowledge, will extend student capacities and enable them to reach high levels of achievement. These processes are demonstrated in the following case example, where the diverse activities involved in the Look–Think–Act routine of action learning provide the means for exciting and energizing student engagement.

Learning Resources

Reflection

1. **Look**: Identify the material in this chapter that describes how action learning provides for experiential and contextual learning that enhances understanding.

   Think: Identify the different sources students may use for gathering information.

   Act: Write a short report describing what decisions students need to make in order to use this information.

2. **Look**: Review the material in this chapter on interviewing.

   Think: Identify the best types of questions to ask informants in order to gather information.

   Act: Choose an issue about teaching or learning in which you are interested. Using the type of questions identified, prepare an interview schedule of questions you would use to interview a colleague or classmate about that issue.

3. **Look**: Review the material in this chapter on the means of documenting student learning.

   Think: Remember a time when you were able to demonstrate what you learned through a nontraditional means as listed in this chapter.

   Act: Write about how you learned from the assessment activity and why you did or did not enjoy it. (Alternatively, use a different means for reporting this information to a group of colleagues or classmates.)

Web Sites

Action Learning:

www.scu.edu.au/schools/gcm/ar/arp/actlearn.html#a_al_al

This site explores the relationship between action research and action learning.

Action Learning Environments in Education:

www.virtualschool.edu/edu/

A collection of information on the use of action learning environments in education to support experiential or interactive learning communities.

Taxonomy of Educational Objectives:

http://faculty.washington.edu/krumme/guides/bloom1.html

www.humboldt.edu/~tha1/bloomtax.html

Annotation. These sites provide extensive information about Bloom's Taxonomy of educational objectives.

Additional Reading

Brockbank, A., & McGill, I. (2003). *The action learning handbook: Powerful techniques for education, professional development and training*. London: Routledge Falmer.

Stringer, E. (2008). *Action research in education*. Upper Saddle River, NJ: Pearson.

NOTES

1. A more detailed exposition of this process is found in *Action Research in Education* (Stringer, 2008, pp. 100–104).

2. A more detailed description of this process is presented in *Action Research in Education* (Stringer, 2008, pp. 104–106).

Assessment and Evaluation

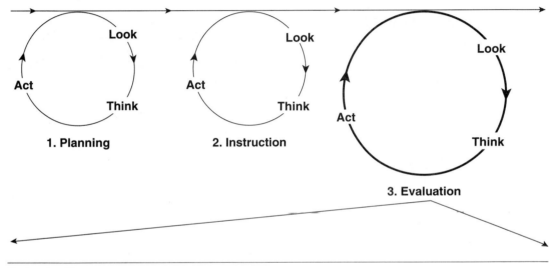

Evaluation Phase

Chapter 6 describes how the Look–Think–Act framework of action research can guide practices of assessment and evaluation.

Assessment

This chapter first shows how assessment procedures can link *student performance* to *state and national standards,* and then shows how *authentic assessment procedure*s can enhance teaching and student learning.

It then provides an overview of *classroom assessment,* describing how it can be used as a *diagnostic tool* to enhance student learning. It also describes a variety of *assessment techniques* that enable students to demonstrate their understanding—questions, tests, learning logs, teacher–student conferences, portfolios, demonstrations, performances, and projects.

The chapter then describes how *formative assessment* procedures can be used to check student progress and learning. It also explains how *summative assessment* techniques demonstrate what students have learned in a lesson. An example of the uses of these techniques is also provided.

Evaluation

The chapter then describes how the Look–Think–Act framework provides teachers with a systematic process to *evaluate their teaching* and *student learning.* This process is then applied to direct instruction and inquiry learning lessons.

ASSESSMENT AND TEACHING

ASSESSMENT: CONSTRUCTIVE AND POSITIVE COMMENTARY

As a teacher, assessment was always a problematic process. When carried out publicly, the less academically talented students in my class always suffered the embarrassment of fumbling for correct answers or having lower test scores revealed. Assessment, I discovered, was best carried out at an individual level where I could provide each student with immediate feedback and, where appropriate, correct information or modeling. "There, Jack," I would say. "See how I carry the 10 into the next column and add it to the other numbers there."

More interesting and rewarding, however, were the times when students presented their projects to the class and, as part of a reflective process, explored the results of their constructions. I could ask them questions like "What do you like about the way you did your project, Melissa?" "What would you do differently if you had the chance to do it again?" These same questions could also be directed at the class. "What did you like about the way Melissa did her project?" "How could she have made it even better?" I modeled constructive and positive commentary so that children could see that the intent was not to punish or sit in judgment, but to provide useful, practical comments that were informative and potentially productive.

Such processes became a positive part of our classroom life, my students enjoying the process of celebrating what they had achieved, while also increasing their understanding of the way to improve their future activities. This, it seemed to me, was the whole purpose of the process of assessment.

—S.B.

Assessment is a central part of classroom life, providing teacher and student with opportunities to monitor the progress of student learning. A balance of formal assessments such as the states' core content assessments with informal assessments that are part of the daily life of a classroom can provide teachers, parents, and policymakers with a more accurate picture of what students are accomplishing in classrooms. Many students view assessment with some degree of apprehension, the judgments of the teacher and the threat of public embarrassment sitting uncomfortably on their shoulders. When used strategically, however, assessment can be a rewarding and productive aspect of schooling, providing students with clear understandings of what, where, and how they can improve their work and offering opportunities to celebrate their accomplishments and classroom productions.

Classroom assessment allows for the presentation of the multiple dimensions of learning through the use of a variety of methods for determining student learning. The emphasis of this text is to engage students in challenging, real-world problem-solving tasks through which they learn to think, process information, and apply what they have learned in different contexts. By engaging them in authentic tasks, students show the process as well as the product of their learning. For example, students demonstrate reading ability with authentic texts rather than contrived passages; they demonstrate their understanding of writing through conferencing with teacher or peers about a piece of their own writing; they construct their understanding of concepts using visual representations and so on. The alignment of standards, outcomes, and assessments we have presented shows that inquiry-based teaching not only addresses interdisciplinary standards but also assesses outcomes through student performance of learning. Although the performance tasks we ask of students do not resemble the state test format, it is not necessary to "teach the test" for students to perform well. Test preparation needs only to introduce students to the test format and provide clarification on what the students will be asked to do.

Assessment therefore needs to be reconsidered, not as a final step of judgment and accountability, but as an integral part of the educational enterprise in which teachers and students are engaged. As they work together to creatively explore the learning processes and opportunities that provide for the future well-being of the students, they turn classroom life into an act of inquiry and discovery that is engaging and life enhancing—that really makes a difference in the lives of students.

MAKING A DIFFERENCE

Most teachers I know want to "make a difference" in the lives of their students, and I have had the wonderful experience of former students telling me of ways that I, as their teacher, have changed their lives through the learning they accomplished under my guidance. This, I feel, is the central core of my work, and one that can be seen and felt at the "heart" of teaching, and the ultimate assessment of the work we have done together.

—S.B.

ASSESSMENT AND ACTION RESEARCH

Traditional models of direct instruction often present assessment as a teacher-focused process (Hunter, 1990/1991; Rosenshine, 1995; Slavin, 2006). Hunter's model incorporates "checking for understanding" before, during, and after a lesson.

As part of the "Teaching/Presentation" phase, teachers check for understanding to determine whether students have "got it," or are "doing it right" before proceeding. Rosenshine's model (1995) includes ongoing "checking for understanding" and "frequent tests" to assess student learning of a skill. Slavin suggests asking relevant questions and giving quizzes to determine level of understanding. Caldwell, Huitt, and French (1981) present a transactional model of direct instruction, where teachers provide a variety of activities to enable students to demonstrate their knowledge and application of concepts or skills learned.

Assessment as part of an inquiry learning cycle tends to place a greater focus on students' engagement in the process of assessing their learning. Particularly in the Expansion phase of the learning cycle, students move through a process of Reviewing, Reflecting, Applying, and Assessing their work. With the assistance of their teachers, students further develop their knowledge and understanding of the extent of their learning.

Applying an action learning/research framework to an assessment process, students first review what they have learned—LOOK. The teacher continues the process by engaging students in reflecting on what they have learned—questioning, clarifying, posing further inquiry—THINK. Finally, students expand on the knowledge gained by applying it in new ways, thus demonstrating the extent of their understanding—ACT (see Figure 6.1). These processes enable students to display their level of understanding of the concept in a number of ways that may be documented in an assessment tool such as a rubric that may be used by the teacher, or by the student for self-assessment.

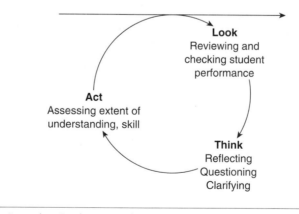

Figure 6.1   Assessing Student Learning

In an effective learning environment, teacher and students share the responsibility of instructional decisions. Teacher planning includes alignment of standards, outcomes, and assessment for every lesson as part of any unit of study. Students as learners need to have a clear understanding of the connection between standards, outcomes, and assessment to the learning task and to state standards-based tests.

Classroom assessment occurs in each lesson, serving as a means for ongoing checks for understanding and advancing student learning and achievement. Teachers help students to use these assessments for self-monitoring and for making decisions about their own learning accomplishments. Together, teachers and students realize how, through challenging, active learning processes, they are meeting the state standards on which students will be tested.

LINKING STUDENT PERFORMANCE AND STATE STANDARDS

INTENT

A brief history of the standards movement will provide readers with the background that will further clarify the intent and contents of this book. Standards have become the driving force across the United States for accountability on both the learning and teaching levels as a result of the 1983 publication *A Nation at Risk: The Imperative for Educational Reform* (National Commission on Excellence in Education, 1983). This government study concluded that schools were failing students and national educational reform was in order. Among its recommendations was the development of measurable standards for determining achievement and setting high expectations for K–16 learners. Despite clear evidence that the report overstated the extent to which schools were responsible for the lower levels of student performance indicated by international comparisons (Berliner & Biddle, 1996), elements of state and national legislatures continued to press for education reform.

In response to these pressures, educational reform during the term of George H. W. Bush became the charge of the state governors. The result of their efforts was the Goals 2000: Educate America Act that was signed into law in 1994 by President Bill Clinton. The intent of Goals 2000 was to provide resources to states and communities to ensure that all students reach their full potential. It established a framework for identifying world-class academic standards, for measuring student progress, and for providing the support that students may need to meet the standards. Specifically, the Goals 2000: Educate America Act states, "All students will leave grades 4, 8, and 12 having demonstrated competency over challenging subject matter . . . and every school in America will ensure that all students will learn to use their minds well, so they may be prepared for responsible citizenship, further learning, and productive employment" (1994). National standards ascertained a level of agreement across the nation on what students should learn and served as a guide for states' development of content and performance standards. Thus, the responsibility for students' learning and achievement remained with the states, districts, and schools.

Goals 2000 laid the groundwork for the No Child Left Behind Act (NCLB) signed into law in 2001 by President George W. Bush. It, among other things, included increased accountability for every state, its districts, and its schools. In addition to establishing a framework of state content standards, every state is required to administer annual standards-based assessments of all children in grades 3–8 that assess students' critical thinking skills in the content areas of language arts literacy, math, and science.

NATIONAL STANDARDS

With the aid of federal dollars, content-related professional organizations developed standards, with the National Council of Teachers of Mathematics (NCTM) leading the way. Standards as written identify specific competencies in the areas of content knowledge and skills at various grade levels. They define what students should know, learn, and be able to do. In general, content standards identify wide-ranging topics that apply to all grade levels. Within each standard are subtopics with learner performance expectations that increase in complexity at each grade level. For example, the New Jersey Core Curriculum Content Standards for Language Arts Literacy has five standards: Reading, Writing, Listening, Speaking, Viewing, and Media Literacy (New Jersey Department of Education, 2004). Each of those standards is divided into strands (subcategories), and each strand includes a list of a varying number of performance indicators for each strand and each grade level. Figure 6.2 provides an example for New Jersey's Language Arts Literacy Standard 3.1 Reading and its strands:

Language Arts Literacy Standard 3.1 Reading—All students will understand and apply the knowledge of sounds, letters, and words in written English to become independent and fluent readers and will read a variety of materials and texts with fluency and comprehension.

Strands K–12:

  A. Concepts About Print
  B. Phonological Awareness
  C. Decoding and Word Recognition
  D. Fluency
  E. Reading Strategies (before, during, and after reading)
  F. Vocabulary and Concept Development
  G. Comprehension Skills and Response to Text
  H. Inquiry and Research

Figure 6.2   A Language Arts Literacy Standard

Standards identified a common set of expectations for all students and were initially developed by professional organizations for each of the core content areas—National

Council of Teachers of Mathematics (NCTM), National Council for the Teaching of English (NCTE), National Council for the Social Studies (NCSS), and American Association for the Advancement of Science (AAAS).

STATE STANDARDS

The national professional organizations' content area standards have served as models for each of the states to develop and revise their own content and performance standards. A glance across other standards of states such as Texas, Illinois, California, New Jersey, and Alabama shows differences in design but similarities in identified competencies. Each state assesses students with criterion-referenced tests that are linked to the state's standards that serve as indicators of levels of student performance.

Although major emphases of these tests across the country have been on math and reading competencies, some states have inserted additional tests for standards-based courses. For example, California requires end-of-course tests in standards-based math courses such as geometry and algebra II as well as history and social science courses. Like California, Texas has end-of-course tests for specific math, English, and history courses. Illinois assesses students in general areas such as fine arts, physical development and health, and social science. Exit-level assessment is also a requirement in most states, testing reading, writing, math, and additional content.

The results of the state standards-based tests are factored in to grade level promotion and high school graduation, and serve as a report card regarding overall school performance, thus becoming "high stakes" tests. In this time of accountability, teachers are under immense pressure to improve student performance. Unfortunately, it has caused many to "teach to the test," their way of feeling assured that they have prepared students for the state tests. It is our contention, however, that this "dumbed down" and deprofessionalized approach to teaching not only serves to alienate teachers and their students from more educationally sound approaches to learning, but that acquisition of standards is better accomplished through active engagement of students in well-planned and creative teaching/learning processes.

Rather than relying on standardized tests as the sole indicators of student achievement and school improvement, there should be a balance between standardized tests *of* learning and classroom assessment *for* learning, thus shifting the focus from what teachers are doing to what students are learning (Stiggins, 2002).

CLASSROOM ASSESSMENT

Technically, classroom assessment is a diagnostic process in which the teacher (and student) evaluates the degree to which the student has learned a piece of knowledge, a concept, or a skill. The student demonstrates his or her knowledge verbally, in writing, or through performing a task or activity. The teacher (and student) evaluates whether or not the student has demonstrated or performed adequately and provides feedback that indicates to the student how to correct or improve his or her performance. The teacher and student LOOK at student demonstration/performance, THINK about the quality of the student work, and ACT to provide feedback or demonstrate correct performance.

Assessment is not merely a mechanical process, however, but a personal and social experience that has a marked impact on the student's experience of learning. Effective assessment procedures enhance student learning experiences by ensuring success and providing the means to achieve a satisfying classroom life. The teacher's task is therefore to develop a range of approaches to assessment that provide students with the means to achieve learning outcomes, while at the same time ensuring that they move systematically through the curriculum.

At the classroom level, teachers develop lesson plans utilizing the state standards as a framework. The teachers align their objectives/learner outcomes and assessments with the state standards they are addressing. They utilize authentic assessment tasks, often with the input of the students, to assess student learning of what is being taught in the classroom. Authentic assessment provides meaningful ways for students to demonstrate their understanding of acquired knowledge by selecting from a choice of activities that replicate challenging, real-world tasks. By offering varied tasks, authentic assessment supports learner differences in the classroom. Teachers use a variety of assessment methods that take into consideration multiple intelligences and learning modalities and capitalize on students' strengths.

Authentic assessment tasks inform students of objectives/outcomes and expectations and may have a number of appropriate answers, as well as including traditional multiple-choice tests for which there is one right answer. Assessment techniques/methods include verbal question/answer, written tests, student learning logs, teacher–student conferences, portfolios, demonstrations, inquiry projects, essay questions, and performances. Scoring tools such as rubrics provide transparent assessment criteria clearly articulating teacher expectations on which the assessment will be measured as well as offering structured feedback. Teachers provide students with the rubrics at the time of assignments so students can prepare their products with the scoring criteria in mind. When students know what is expected, they are better able to create in-depth, rational responses, performances, or products.

Formative and Summative Assessment

Formative and summative assessments are two major procedures for teachers to document student learning, to evaluate the quality and extent of student learning, and to analyze the effectiveness of their teaching. *Formative assessment* checks for students' understanding and progress as an ongoing part of a lesson and is used as a way to advance learning (Stiggins, Arter, & Chappuis, 2007). These progress checks are an integral part of the lesson and can take many forms. For example, teachers engage in "kidwatching" (Goodman, 1978), or observations, and make mental notes, write anecdotal notes, or complete a checklist. Various learning strategies can inform teachers of prior knowledge, understanding, and progress for both individual students and student groups. For example, the use of the Group Mapping Activity allows student groups to demonstrate their understanding of a concept by collaboratively constructing a visual map and explaining their construction to the teacher or class. Quick Writes and Learning Logs can serve as self-assessments for students to reflect on their own learning through writing as well as informing the teacher of student understanding and where there is a need for clarification or reteaching. The value placed on formative assessments is determined by their purpose. Oftentimes, it is stated in terms of completion or an accumulated value. For example, a checklist may indicate completion of a task. In the direct instruction lesson on persuasive speeches in Chapter 3, the teacher indicated throughout the lesson tasks that would serve as formative assessments or progress checks, informing her of student understanding. Figure 6.3 is an example of a checklist that the teacher might use to assess the content of her students' speeches while they are in the process of preparing them:

Item	Yes	No
1. Opened with a "hook"		
2. Chose understandable/ unambiguous vocabulary		
3. Used appropriately facts, opinions		
4. Used supportive details		
5. Remained focused on topic		
6. Demonstrated knowledge and understanding of topic		

Figure 6.3   Formative Assessment of a Speech

Summative assessment, on the other hand, is the final product or culminating activity that demonstrates what students have learned as a result of the lesson or unit. To assess, teachers might utilize a scoring tool or rubric that clearly identifies the criteria for the successful performance—that which is to be assessed and the level of proficiency—aligning the criteria with the stated learner outcomes and state standards of the lesson/unit. Rubric formats can vary depending on the items being assessed, and may include task dimensions with listed criteria, possible points, and a point scale. Some examples are analytic scales, holistic scoring scales, structured observational instruments, students' self-assessments, and portfolio assessments.

By adding numerical value and a list of criteria to the speech checklist above, it becomes an analytic scoring scale as shown in Figure 6.4. It lists the criteria being assessed and the numerical determination for accomplishing each criterion. The teacher would provide this rubric to her students as they begin to prepare their own speeches to present to the class.

Collaborations between teachers and students to design and utilize assessment tools are highly productive, placing students in a position where they have ownership of and responsibility for their own learning. When students are asked to assess their own learning, they have to think about their own learning processes for acquiring new knowledge.

Item	1	2	3
1. Opened with a "hook"	"Hookless"	Introduced topic but lacked "hook"	"Hook" gained audience attention
2. Chose understandable/ unambiguous vocabulary	Vocabulary choices hard to understand, follow	Vocabulary choices understandable but sometimes ambiguous	Vocabulary choices understandable and unambiguous
3. Used appropriately facts, opinions	Did not use facts/opinions appropriately	Did use facts/opinions appropriately but opinions dominant	Used facts and opinions appropriately and well-balanced
4. Used supportive details to make points	Did not use supportive details	Did use some supportive details	Well-supported points
5. Remained focused on topic	Lost focus	Remained focused most of the time	Clearly focused throughout
6. Demonstrated knowledge and understanding of topic	Lacked knowledge and clear understanding of topic	Demonstrated knowledge and understanding of topic	Well-informed and clear understanding of topic

Figure 6.4 Summative Assessment of a Speech

**RECOGNIZING GROWTH AND
PROGRESS THROUGH ASSESSMENT**

As a reading and ESL teacher in a high school in the metropolitan area of Houston, Texas, I taught many ELL students. For new arrivals in an ESL reading course, I incorporated a kind of portfolio task as an assessment. The students housed all of their written work such as journal entries and major reading and writing assignments in a folder that was kept in a file box in the classroom. The students assisted me in creating a self-assessment tool for evaluating their progress in the acquisition of English. Toward the end of the fall and spring semesters, I engaged the students in reflecting on what we had done during the semester. Their verbal recollections along with the papers in their folders provided them with artifacts to evaluate their English language literacy progress. Their task was to select the following:

1. A favorite assignment

2. An assignment they liked and learned a lot

3. Least favorite but learned much from it

4. One additional assignment of their choice

For each of these assignments, they were to assign a numerical grade between 1 (low) and 5 (high), and were given guidelines for responding in writing why they assigned the numerical score and why they chose each particular assignment.

I wish I could have captured on film the moments when these students were going through their folders. They reread every paper thoughtfully; they laughed to themselves and with others as they shared with peers; some shed a few tears as they perused journal entries. What was most revealing to them as they reflected on their work from semester's beginning to end was the English language they had acquired. Their self-efficacy reached new heights! I learned from these students how important it is to guide students toward seeing their own progress and enabling them to identify their areas for growth. Too often, students can only see what they can't do or haven't learned. They don't pay attention to how they have progressed.

—S.B.

EVALUATION

Utilization of the Look–Think–Act cycle within lessons of both direct instruction and inquiry provides teachers with a systematic process through which to evaluate *their own teaching success in relation to overall student learning*. The teachers review their lessons looking at the levels of student performance on both the formative assessments and summative assessment to check for learning and understanding. From this analysis, they determine the strengths of the class, areas to improve, evidence of gaps in learning, and what action to take to remediate.

The assessments described in the following lessons provide multiple examples of formative and summative assessment. The teachers were able to follow the progress of their students by embedding different kinds of formative assessment throughout the phases of their lessons. These formative assessments provided an "audit trail" connecting learner outcomes, standards, and assessments. In doing so, they are monitoring student understanding of the subject matter and assessing their own success in addressing the standards and achieving the learner outcomes they had set for the lesson.

Each iteration of assessment also required a small cycle of inquiry through which the students and teachers evaluated their activity. They would:

- **Look** at the work that had been done,

- **Think** about the quality of the work—what was right with it, what needed improving or correcting, and

- **Act** to correct or improve their performance.

An Assessment Process: Outcomes > Standards > Learning Activities > Assessment Tasks

Evaluation of a Direct Instruction Lesson

Preparation

In preparing the first phases of the persuasive speech lessons (see Chapter 3, p. 43, and Chapter 4, p. 83), the teacher identified learner outcomes, state performance standards, the learning activities, and the assessment tasks that would demonstrate student progress and level of achievement of the learner outcomes and, ultimately, the state standards. The teacher evaluated her lessons by cyclically working through an action research process at regular intervals:

Presentation

Look: She applied questioning as a pre-assessment to focus students' attention and connect to what they already knew about the art of persuasion. After teaching the students the key elements, she provided students a speech handout and asked them to label those elements.

Think: At this point, she checked for understanding by asking students how they labeled different aspects of the speech. From their responses, she was able to determine the need for re-teaching for clarification and understanding.

Practice

Act: To prepare their own speeches, students constructed webs as a means for outlining their topic. This visual allowed the teacher to see student progress and offer assistance individually as needed. For homework, the students had to prepare a rough draft of their speech from their web for class the next day.

Presentation

Look: Assessing for learning continued the next day with the rough drafts of the students' speeches.

Think: The teacher asked the students to identify with a star the effective elements of persuasion in their own speeches.

Practice

Act: Another formative assessment followed with student partners reading their speeches to each other. The teacher, while circulating, was able to intervene where assistance was needed.

The teacher applied the same process in teaching her students about effective persuasive speaking, the second phase of the lesson, by pre-assessing their knowledge. Following a mini-lecture on effective persuasive speaking (**Look**), she checked for understanding by having students identify key elements of effective speaking in two videotaped speeches (**Think**). The guided practice phase of the lesson involved students practicing their speeches with an assigned partner (**Act**). The teacher informally assessed their application of effective speaking as they practiced.

As a summative assessment, each student presented his or her speech to the class. The teacher assessed each student for elements of both effective persuasion and speaking, aligning with the identified learner outcomes and standards. In addition, students and teacher assessed the adequacy of the graphic organizer and the speech script. They identified strengths of the organizer/script, and weaknesses, errors, or deficiencies. Finally, the teacher provided a written assessment and commentary on each student's work, based on the extent to which and the ways the student had achieved the lesson outcomes. By reviewing these assessments, she was able to *evaluate* the quality of her own teaching, identifying the extent to which the class had achieved stipulated objectives and outcomes, and points at which she could enhance her instruction.

EVALUATION OF AN INQUIRY LEARNING LESSON

For Mr. W's environmental science class (see Appendix, p. 172), his stated goal for the course is, "For my students to realize as citizens, they have both a responsibility to their community and a voice in the decisions made about their community." His rationale for the introductory lesson was to connect to his course goal by bringing the course into his students' backyards, relating their learning to the way local environmental issues affected them and their community. Then the course would expand toward a more global perspective.

EXPLORATION

Look: Mr. W realized that in order to draw his students into the course topic of environmental science, he would need to make it relevant to them. Contextualizing it in their own community was an excellent starting point. Through the use of a community master plan map, he was able to illustrate a real issue of choice of land use. Probing questions served as a pre-assessment of what the students knew about the topic and activated students' thinking. He was able to determine their knowledge level about decision making concerning community environmental issues and to connect their understandings to what they were going to be learning.

 Think: He asked students to identify environmental issues that impact their lives in their community and to choose one of the identified topics of interest to research.

 Act: He was able to determine student understanding and the level of engagement.

DEVELOPMENT

Look: The collaborative creation of group concept maps on their selected environmental issue required students to put in writing their group understanding and to organize their thinking about their topic. Their creation of a visual schematic of their thinking served as a point of departure. The visual display created by each group served as a formative assessment, a way to check for group understanding and progress.

 Think: Further culling of information through critical analysis, and multiple revisions of the group's concept map, demonstrated students' accommodation for new knowledge and better understanding. Mr. W could monitor these changes while walking from group to group and noting the activity. At this time he was able to clarify and "re-teach" as needed.

Act: The students acted on the information they were gathering and the knowledge they were acquiring by preparing presentations for their peers. Each group presented its issue to the whole class, which assessed this activity using a rubric constructed by the teacher and students. This served as a summative assessment, informing the teacher about student understanding and attentiveness, and the presenters' quality of their presentation.

EXPANSION

Look: As students reflected on their peers' assessments, they determined their level of success for informing their peers about their topics. Mr. W learned from the assessments the level of knowledge acquired through the activities, which helped him to determine his level of success in teaching.

Think: Quick Writes, another formative assessment, allowed the students an opportunity to reflect on their learning while simultaneously providing Mr. W with a snapshot of the level of learning. Discussions were an additional barometer for determining level of learning, however, not as accurate as not all students participated.

Act: To further demonstrate their knowledge about specific environmental issues and to share the information outside the classroom, the students prepared a plan that included the rationale, the identified audience, and an outline of the presentation and the format to be used. The plan provided another summative assessment that will involve both self-assessment and teacher assessment.

Utilization of a self-assessment tool is very informative to both the student and the teacher in determining the level of learning and strengths and areas needing improvement or clarification. Mr. W had incorporated numerous activities as formative and summative assessments from which to identify areas of strength, need for improvement in instruction, and the alignment of standards, outcomes, and assessments.

Once again the Look–Think–Act cycle provided the teachers with a structure through which to evaluate their lessons. Teachers went through the process of reviewing the lessons, analyzing and evaluating the overall outcomes, and planning for needed remediation.

CONCLUSION

The Look–Think–Act action research cycle provides teachers with a structure through which they can assess student outcomes and evaluate the effectiveness of their instruction. It enables teachers and students to clearly define the processes of systematically reviewing their progress, assessing their success in attaining the objectives they wish to achieve, and acting to remediate inadequate performance or celebrating successful achievement. Processes of formative assessment enable teacher and students to monitor their progress throughout a lesson, providing opportunities for students to improve or extend their learning. Final summative assessments enable teacher and students to evaluate the outcomes of the lesson, assessing the degree to which they have successfully achieved the objectives of the lesson. This information also enables teachers to evaluate the effectiveness of their own instruction, and to note areas of weakness that will need to be addressed in future lessons.

LEARNING RESOURCES

Reflection

1. **Look**: A big concern for teachers is being held accountable for student learning that often results in "teaching to the test." Identify elements of an action research model that provides teachers with assurance that they are "covering all the bases."

   Think: Assessment should be an integral part of the lesson design. It should be both formative and summative. Select two examples of formative assessments and two examples of summative assessments from the lessons provided in this book. Explain your understanding of how each of these assessments allows teachers (and students) to determine their level of understanding and learning or to advance student learning.

   Act: When observation is insufficient as a means for assessment, the teacher then must move to short conversations or discussion. What does a teacher's behavior look like in the classroom when engaging learners in short conversation? What are the roles of the teacher?

2. **Look**: What recollections do you have about the kinds of assessments used to grade your performance as a student?

   Think The role of reflection as part of a lesson is a critical piece for both the teacher and the students. From your own experiences as a student, were you asked to engage in reflecting on your own learning? If so, what did that look like? If not, how did you evaluate your own learning? Or how did you think about your own learning? How is this highlighted in the action research lesson cycle?

   Act What did you learn about your own learning from these assessments? What did you do with this information?

Web Sites

Kathy Schrock's Guide for Educators: Assessment and Rubric Information
http://school.discovery.com/schrockguide/assess.html

Extensive information about assessment tools to be used by both teachers and students for formative and summative assessment.

Rubrics 4 Teachers

http://rubrics4teachers.com

A complete guide for educational rubrics categorized by subject, application variations, levels, and rubric construction tools.

The Technology Applications Center for Educator Development

www.tcet.unt.edu/START/instruct/general/rubrics.htm

An informative site with definition of rubrics, their utilization for assessment of technology skills, technology products, general use, and construction examples.

4 Teachers.org

http://pblchecklist.4teachers.org/checklists.html

Specific to project-based checklists, provides teachers with tools to construct checklists for grade levels in writing, science, oral presentation, and multimedia.

Internet 4 Classrooms: Teacher Tools

www.internet4classrooms.com/teachertools.htm

Offers numerous links for quiz- and test-writing tips, and assessment tools such as rubrics.

Scholastic Teaching Resources

http://teacher.scholastic.com/professional/assessment/indexbk.htm

Examples of graphic organizers and rubric makers for evaluation of student work.

Additional Reading

Berliner, D. C., & Biddle, B. J. (1996). *The manufactured crisis: Myths, fraud, and the attack on American schools.* Reading, MA: Addison-Wesley Publishing.

Goodman, Y. (1978). Kidwatching: An alternative to testing. *National Elementary Principal, 57,* 41–45.

Goals 2000: Educate America Act of 1994, Pub. L. No. 103-227, (1994).

Helms, A., Graeber, J., Caldwell, J., & Huitt, W. (Eds.). (1981). *Basic skills instructional improvement program: Leader's guide for student engaged time.* Philadelphia: Research for Better Schools.

Hunter, M. (December 1990/January 1991). Hunter lesson design helps achieve the goals of science instruction. *Educational Leadership, 48*(4), 79–81.

National Commission on Excellence in Education. (1983). *A nation at risk: The imperative for educational reform.* Washington, DC: U.S. Department of Education.

No Child Left Behind Act of 2001, Pub. L. No. 107-110, 115 Stat. 1425 (2002).

Rosenshine, B. (1995). Advances in research on instruction. *Journal of Educational Research, 88*(5), 261–268.

Slavin, R. (1997). *Educational psychology* (5th ed.). Boston: Allyn and Bacon.

Stiggins, R. (2002). Assessment crisis: The absence of assessment FOR learning. *Phi Delta Kappan, 80*(10), 758–765. Retrieved June 2, 2007, from ProQuest database.

Stiggins, R., Arter, J., & Chappuis, J. (2007). *Classroom assessment for student learning.* Educational Testing Service.

Appendix

Case Examples

This chapter presents three case examples of lessons that use the Look–Think–Act action research process to guide teacher instruction, student learning, and assessment and evaluation. The lessons include:

- An integrated lesson on sea life for Grade 1 students that incorporates standards from science, social studies, mathematics, and literacy. It demonstrates how action research and action learning processes can provide students with a wide range of activities that enable them to work across the curriculum.

- An integrated community life lesson for Grades 5 and 7 that incorporates standards from language arts literacy and social studies. It provides a clear indication of the way that classroom activities can be made relevant to the community experience of diverse students.

- A lesson on environmental decision making for a high school class that incorporates standards from social studies, science, and language arts literacy. This plan demonstrates how carefully planned learning activities provide the means for students to accomplish outcomes directly associated with a set of state standards.

Case Example A.1: A Lesson on Sea Life

The following lesson illustrates the ways that the Look–Think–Act action research sequence provided the means for the teacher, Ellen Stubblefield, to organize and keep track of the sea life lesson with her first-grade class. This is an integrative study that covered a 6-week period and provided students with multiple opportunities to engage diverse and interesting learning activities relevant to their age and stage of development.

The lesson plan is followed by a Teacher Reflection that provided the opportunity for Ms. Stubblefield to reflect on the lesson, to identify points of strength and weakness, and to review the extent to which she had been able to accomplish the associated standards. The lesson is an extended interdisciplinary learning project in which all class members assisted Ms. Stubblefield to design the lesson, using authentic learning experiences to actively explore the topic through a challenging yet relevant array of learning strategies. Meaningful assessments emerged as students created and produced many different types of products to demonstrate they had achieved learning outcomes. This lesson offers a clear model of the way action learning/action research processes can be applied to a learning project for early childhood learners.

As Ms. Stubblefield's reflections reveal, her high levels of organization enabled students to work effectively in a safe and supportive learning environment. Students were very task oriented, understood the carefully organized classroom routines, and gave their teacher few behavioral problems. Varied instructional strategies, including cooperative groups, carefully prepared learning centers, appropriate technology, role-playing, guest speakers, field trips, and choral reading aroused and maintained the first graders' interest throughout the lesson. By implementing instructional strategies closely aligned with action learning and research, Ms. Stubblefield and her first graders were able to achieve a full range of learning outcomes. These included:

- Achieving state and national standards in all of the content areas of the curriculum
- Developing high levels of skill
- Developing high levels of concept development
- Developing interesting and useful generalizations
- Exhibiting autonomous learning
- Making effective decisions
- Thinking critically
- Applying inquiry processes
- Achieving social action
- Learning cooperative processes
- Developing, utilizing, and enhancing technology skills
- Defending hypotheses about particular concepts or generalizations

Primary students were able to achieve these outcomes by making use of a wide array of learning strategies and resources:

- Community personnel and resources
- Aesthetics were a part of the curriculum.
- Young learners evaluated their own learning. (Christensen, Stubblefield, & Watson, 2008).

At parent–teacher conferences, numerous student work samples provided evidence of how much students had learned:

- Digital photos captured student learning processes and outcomes.
- Parents participated in classroom learning.

Youngsters assisted bilingual students with English as a second language, students with special needs, and students who were struggling with reading, writing, or numeracy. The integrated nature of the learning processes enabled cognitive, social, and affective goals to be incorporated into the lesson. These young, diverse learners were able to accomplish an in-depth study and cover the required curriculum in every area prescribed by the state and national standards. They spent 6 weeks of in-depth study, starting with small learning activities and expanding to meet the full range of standards. Cooperative and collaborative learning provided many opportunities to engage broad, purposeful topics that were relevant to the students' interests and experiences. Active involvement in planning, research, and evaluation provided multiple opportunities for development that were not only relevant but active, rigorous, and challenging, and extended to families and the rest of their schoolmates.

Topic: Sea Life

Subjects: Science, Social Studies, Mathematics, and Literacy

Grade: First Grade

Duration: Integrated activities over a period of 6 weeks

Standards: See end of lesson plan.

Materials

Globes, paper, pencils

Book review and data sheets for recording information

Writing journals

Fiction and nonfiction texts, Internet searches, interviews with a local pet store owner and a college professor expert on Antarctica

Photos and digital photo information on their topics

Cardboard boxes

String

Colored construction paper

Plastic wrap

(Continued)

(Continued)

Glue sticks

Trifold paper

Bubble wrap

Colored markers

Books: *How Many Days to America?* by Eve Bunting (1988) and J. Pollata's (2000) *Dory Story*

Likert scale evaluative tool (teacher created)

Special Needs Modifications: One-on-one instruction if necessary, peer tutors, provide step-by-step instructions, have appropriate reading materials, check on progress regularly, have an aide and assistive technology if possible, work with a special educator to modify instruction

Bilingual English Language Learner Strategies: Peer tutors; labels in student(s)' language; word walls in native tongue and English; adapted texts; instructions and directions in representative/native language if possible; utilization of visuals such as pictorial schematics, graphic organizers, charts to illustrate concepts, directions, and so on

---

Phase 1   Exploration

Objectives/ outcomes	Teacher instruction	Student learning	Assessment
Objectives The students will identify what they know about sea life observing globes for the oceans and landmasses and record information. **Standards** *Literacy: 4.* Demonstrate understanding of letter–sound relationships. Using decoding skills. Blending sounds to form words.	**Look** The teacher will ask students to recall a topic of study from the previous academic year. She gives each group of three a globe. She asks each group to answer the following question in their writing journals, "Where is the ocean?" She asks the children, "What lives in the ocean?" **Think** Each group's charge is to list or draw the types of sea animals that they know about that live in the ocean. The students process the questions through thinking and processing information about what they know by brainstorming (talking and writing) about sea animals.	**Look** Primary students identify what they know about sea life in small groups using globes to help them think about landmasses, oceans, and seas. Groups of three examine the globe and look at the seas and oceans to help them think about the teacher's questions. **Think** Students think about and discuss all of the types of life that they know that live in the sea. One student in the group is the recorder. That student writes down all of the suggestions about sea life from the brainstorming session.	Lists in journals that identify what groups of students know about sea life from observations of globes to prompt thinking about the ocean.

Objectives/ outcomes	Teacher instruction	Student learning	Assessment
Social Studies: 6. Identify features of Earth as landmasses or bodies of water.	**Act** The students record in a list as many types of sea life as possible that they know.	**Act** Together, each group reads over their list of sea life and adds to the list other types.	

Phase 2   Development

Materials

Book review and data sheets for recording information

Writing journals

Fiction and nonfiction texts

Internet searches

Interviews with a local pet store owner and a college professor expert on Antarctica

Photos and digital photo information on their topics

Cardboard boxes

String

Colored construction paper

Plastic wrap

Glue sticks

Trifold paper

Bubble wrap

Colored markers

Objectives/ outcomes	Teacher instruction	Student learning	Assessment
Students observe, research, and record the places and types of sea animals, plants, creatures, and birds that live in sea habitats.	**Look** The teacher asks student groups to respond to questions about sea animals. The teacher records students' answers on a large paper chart. **Think** The teacher asks further questions to assist children to extend their thinking about sea animals. "What do you already know about sea life?" "What else do you want to know?" "Where do we find answers to our questions?"	**Look** Students focus on sea animals at the teacher's request. Students suggest sea animals and the teacher records suggestions on chart paper. **Think** Through questioning, the teacher extends children's thinking about sea animals. Groups choose particular animals on which to focus research. Groups explore teacher questions.	Book review and data sheets for students to use for recording gathered information about topics.

(Continued)

Phase 2 (Continued)

Objectives/ outcomes	Teacher instruction	Student learning	Assessment
	Act The teacher finishes recording the students' responses. She asks the children to help her reorganize and group responses. She asks students to develop headings for each group that make sense to them for the areas of study.	**Act** From the recorded responses, and the chosen areas of research, first-grade groups start choosing from the texts set aside in the classroom for gathering information.	
	Look The students and the teacher decide where they can look for information about research on each of the chosen topics.	**Look** Groups have a list of where they can gather information for chosen topics of sea animals. Each group member gathers particular resources about their topic.	
	Think The teacher questions the students, "Where will we find out about sea plants?" "Is there someone who could tell us perhaps about sea birds and animals?" "What types of books might have information about living sea animals and creatures?" She asks the students to look at globes again to see all the coastlines and to name all of the different oceans and seas. Again, the teacher poses questions about where they might find out about some of these places and types of sea animals, plants, creatures, and birds that live in sea habitats. The teacher requests that students discuss research and information for their chosen topics using the resources identified.	**Think** Students rethink sea plants, birds, animals, and other creatures. They look at coastlines, oceans, and seas to prompt thinking about habitats. Students will include this information in their research. Students begin discussing information and documenting research on sticky notes and on book review sheets about their topics.	

Objectives/ outcomes	Teacher instruction	Student learning	Assessment
	Act The teacher creates a preset basic type of "book review" sheet for students to record information. Each group records information and documents whether a book was fiction or nonfiction or an Internet reference was used (partner readers with nonreaders).	**Act** Students develop questions, listen, and take notes, as a professor from a local university comes and discusses his expertise about Antarctica and its animals, birds, habitats, fish, and so on.	
	The teacher asks students to decide how to document what and how they learned about sea life and how to protect it.	The students decide to display what they have learned by creating aquariums. Each group creates an aquarium. They take boxes and, with help, cut out large ovals on each side. They measure with string to find the middle of each side and cut a hole in each side. They cover each hole with clear plastic wrap. They cut paper sea animals and plants and put sea life inside and decorate the outside with quotes about what they have learned. Students record habitats for each living animal with photos and written comments. They place these in front of their aquariums for display.	Aquariums created from boxes document what students learned about sea life.
	The teacher asks students to display their aquariums.	Students display their aquariums.	
	The teacher asks each group to construct a brochure about jellyfish and make jellyfish out of bubble wrap.	Groups create brochures about jellyfish and create jellyfish with bubble wrap. Brochures and jellyfish were displayed on a bulletin board outside of the classroom in the hallway for viewing by other students, parents, teachers, or visitors.	Trifold brochures about dangers and advantages of jellyfish record student learning.

Phase 3   Expansion

Materials			
How Many Days to America? by Eve Bunting (1988) and J. Pollata's (2000) *Dory Story.* Likert scale evaluative tool (teacher created)			
Objectives/ outcomes	*Teacher instruction*	*Student learning*	*Assessment*
The students will evaluate what they have learned about sea life. They will also evaluate the process of learning about sea life and re-search to create a script for a play.	**Look** The teacher asks students to reflect and evaluate the entire process and project on sea life by going over each one of their research documents.		**Look** The teacher and the students reflect and evaluate the entire process and project on sea life by going over each one of their research documents.
	Think Teacher asks each student what he or she thought about the sea life learning project. Teacher asks students to create and perform a play that demonstrates what they learned about sea life.	**Act** Students respond to the teacher. **Look** Each group reviews learning materials created for the sea life project. **Think** They select key elements and use that information to create a script. Volunteer parents create sets for the play. **Act** Each group performs a play about sea life.	**Think** They evaluate each part of the process using a Likert scale with smiley faces for preference indication. **Act** Teacher records their responses, observations, and further research. **Evaluation** **Look** As students perform their plays, the teacher observes and reads notes she has taken during the lesson. Parents attend the play as well as other schoolmates. **Think** She identifies ways in which she could have improved students' activities to more effectively meet the curriculum standards.

Alabama State Course of Study Standards: Sea Life Lesson

Alabama State Course of Study Standards: Science

Earth and Space Science

Students will:

8. Identify features of Earth as landmasses or bodies of water.

Physical Science

Students will:

1. Select appropriate tools and technological resources needed to gather, analyze, and interpret data.

2. Identify basic properties of objects—size, shape, color, texture.

Life Science

Students will:

4. Describe survival traits of living things, including color, shape, size, texture, and covering:
   - Classify plants and animals according to physical traits.
   - Identify developmental stages of plants and animals.
   - Describe a variety of habitats and natural homes of animals.

Alabama State Course of Study Standards: Social Studies

Social Studies

Students will:

1. Identify past and present modes of air, land, and water transportation.
   - Identifying primary documents of the past and present

2. Describe how primary sources serve as historical records of families and communities.

3. Identify historical events and celebrations in communities and cities throughout Alabama.

5. Label human-made and natural resources in Alabama.

6. Identify landmasses, bodies of water, and other physical features of Earth on maps and globes.

7. Identify ways to take personal action to protect the environment.

10. Discuss civic responsibilities of a participating member of a community and state.

ALABAMA STATE COURSE OF STUDY: MATHEMATICS

Students will:

8. Differentiate among plane shapes, including circles, squares, rectangles, and triangles.
   - Describing similarities and differences between plane and solid shapes
   - Transferring shape combinations from one representation (dimension) to another
   - Recognizing real-life examples of line symmetry
   - Changing the position of objects or shapes by sliding (translation) and turning (rotation)
   - Combining shapes to fill in the area of a given shape

9. Identify solid shapes in the environment, including cubes, rectangular prisms, cones, spheres, and cylinders.

10. Compare objects according to length, weight, and capacity.
    - Measuring the length of objects using a variety of nonstandard units
    - Using objects of equal length—comparing number of equally sized paper clips needed to measure length of desk
    - Ordering according to attributes

ALABAMA STATE COURSE OF STUDY STANDARDS: LITERACY

Students will:

9. Demonstrate reading improvement gained through substantial amounts of daily reading.

11. Read orally with accuracy, fluency, and comprehension.

- Making self-corrections
- Reading with expression
- Applying mental operations involved in comprehension

Examples: make inferences, relate to prior experience, recognize cause and effect, draw conclusions

12. Demonstrate an interest in and enjoyment of literature in a variety of forms and contexts.

- Selecting books for enjoyment and knowledge
- Sharing books and ideas encountered in print and other media
- Using books and media responsibly
- Using expanded vocabulary in speaking and writing

13. Connect knowledge learned in the language arts program to life situations.

Examples: comparing characters or events in a story to people or events in real life, making lists

14. Apply study strategies.

- Alphabetizing
- Identifying parts of books
- Classifying
- Summarizing
- Using test-taking strategies
- Interpreting charts and graphs

16. Demonstrate appropriate listening and speaking behaviors.

- Focusing on the listening task

Examples: conversation, instruction, group discussion, read-alouds

- Establishing eye contact with the speaker or audience
- Interpreting nonverbal communication of the speaker or audience

Example: facial expressions

- Asking appropriate questions to gain and to clarify information
- Attending to works of literature presented orally

17. Exhibit expanded sentence awareness and vocabulary.

- Participating in shared reading and writing

Examples: choral reading, big books, journals, language experience

- Responding to questions

Examples: elements of a story, fact and fantasy, appropriate conclusion, simple sequence of events

- Asking questions for clarification
- Engaging in word-study activities

Examples: synonyms, antonyms, homonyms, multiple-meaning words, concept mapping and webbing, context clues

19. Begin to use conventional mechanics and spelling when editing written expression.
    - Capitalizing proper nouns, titles of people, first word in a sentence
    - Punctuating with periods and question marks as end marks
    - Spelling correctly three- and four-letter, short-vowel words

20. Apply proper use of grammar for written and spoken communication.
    - Nouns
    - Verbs
    - Subject–verb agreement with simple subject

21. Use writing as a tool for expressing thoughts in all disciplines.

    Examples: lists, thank-you notes, journals, science and mathematics logs, friendly letters, envelopes

22. Write using manuscript.
    - Developing letter formation of upper- and lowercase letters
    - Spacing appropriate

TEACHER REFLECTION: EVALUATION

An action research cycle also assisted Ms. Stubblefield to evaluate the overall effectiveness of this lesson.

LOOK

She reviewed all of the learning activities in which the students had engaged, and the processes by which she had facilitated them. She also reviewed the outcomes of those activities, and the quality of those outcomes. This provided the information she needed to identify the state standards her students had been able to accomplish, and the level of their performance.

THINK

This information enabled her to identify many ways in which other aspects of the curriculum could enhance or be enhanced by the sea life project. Taking each set of the standards, she found areas that were overlooked, and recorded questions to ask the first graders. Questions would serve as prompts for further research that would meet the standards.

ACT

In immediate terms she was able to extend the work of the project to other areas of the curriculum. She implemented lessons where the children worked mathematics problems about the blubber of blue whales and the number of tentacles on jellyfish. The students wrote stories in their journals about sharks, sea beasts, and mermaids. They studied the careers of marine biologists, offshore drillers, shrimpers, oceanographers, and divers. Even their palettes enjoyed sea star sandwiches and cheese cracker fish. They studied the water cycle and made models of it. The students prompted most of these ideas, and Ms. Stubblefield simply nudged them further.

Ms. Stubblefield also evaluated the lesson by reviewing the NCTE/IRA, NCSS, NCTM, and NSTA standards and the State Courses of Study Standards in literacy, math, social studies, and science to see where she actually met each particular standard item and where she might have areas in which to grow. The use of anecdotal records was her means to document the areas of success and those where she fell short, providing her with a summative evaluation of the lesson.

This evaluation demonstrates how the processes of action research—**LOOK, THINK, AND ACT**—are cyclical in nature, and embedded within the phases of an inquiry learning lesson. Research in the first grade encompassed the entire curriculum and was student centered. It was a minds- and hands-on experience. Ms. Stubblefield was a participant and a guide in the process of learning, as were the parents and other teachers and children in the school.

Case Example A.2: Community Life—A Commercial Project

Previous chapters described lessons in terms of a Look–Think–Act action research process that provides teachers with an organized way to plan, review, and evaluate their teaching and student learning. This case example shows how the teacher used this process to keep track of the complexities of a complex project that includes student learning activities, curriculum content, evaluation procedures, and performance standards. The lesson shows how students can be included as active participants in planning and assessing their own learning—to think about their own thinking and understand how they learn. It takes them beyond preparation for a test, to preparation for their place in the world. Through systematic inquiry, students begin to understand that they have their own understanding of the world, and as they are given opportunities to explore, investigate, and discover, they acquire new knowledge that adds to or alters their schema.

In this study, preservice teachers learned about teaching, learning, and diversity in an urban service learning experience as they guided the students through an inquiry project utilizing the action research model LOOK–THINK–ACT (Stringer, 2008) as a pedagogical process. This action research model provided preservice teachers with a simple, systematic means for actively engaging their student partners in a project that was relevant to their lives and met the curriculum and state performance standards.

As preservice teachers, they were in control, enacting this pedagogical approach and seeing firsthand their students' responses. The preservice teachers and students worked in a cooperative partnership to plan each meeting in order to accomplish their goal. In the process, a sense of community emerged in which there was respect for and validation of all participants' thoughts and opinions. The preservice teachers were able to connect action research and action learning for investigating their students' real world. They applied learning strategies from course content for structuring and organizing information offered by the students. Through systematic reflection, they gained insight into their own thinking about the academic, social, and emotional aspects of learning and became aware of differences (not deficits) in learners.

The commercial project was invaluable not only to the preservice teachers, but also to their student partners, as revealed in their final assessments. Preservice teachers developed assessment tools to enable the students to evaluate the project. One group used the List–Group–Label strategy as an assessment tool, while other groups had prepared open-ended questions to which their students responded. Their analysis of the students' responses revealed that the students had benefited academically, socially, and emotionally from the project. For example, some students noted improvement in their reading, writing, and speaking skills and recognized the importance of organization. They commented repeatedly about learning to work together and to cooperate with one another. Finally, the students felt a sense of accomplishment and achievement of making a difference in their community by highlighting its attractions. The essence of this was captured in a seventh-grade student's evaluative comment: "We accomplished our goals and we did it ourselves. This makes me happy!"

Topic: A Commercial Project

Lesson: Community Life

Grade: Years Five and Seven

Duration: Six 75-minute sessions

New Jersey State Standards

Social Studies

6.4.8 U.S. and NJ History

A. Family and Community Life

Language Arts Literacy

Reading

3.1.7G Comprehension

3.1.5, 7H Inquiry and Research

Writing

3.2.5A Writing as a Process

3.2.5, 7D Writing Forms, Audiences, and Purposes

Speaking

3.3.5, 7A Discussion

3.3.5, 7B Questioning and Contributing

3.3.5, 7D Oral Presentations

Listening

3.4.5, 7A Active Listening

3.4.5, 7B Listening Comprehension

Viewing

3.5.5, 7A Constructing Meaning

3.5.5B Visual and Verbal Messages

Accommodations/Modifications: One-on-one instruction if necessary, peer tutors, provide step-by-step instructions, have appropriate reading materials, check on progress regularly, have an aide and assistive technology if possible, work with a special educator to modify instruction

Bilingual English Language Learner Strategies: Peer tutors; labels in student(s)' language; word walls in native tongue and English; adapted texts; instructions and directions in representative/native language if possible; utilization of visuals such as pictorial schematics, graphic organizers, charts to illustrate concepts, directions, and so on

Phase 1   Exploration

Objectives/ outcomes	Teacher instruction	Student learning	Assessment
Students will: Identify outcomes of previous project. Demonstrate ability to work cooperatively in groups.	**Look** Teacher asks, "What do you remember from last summer's project with your college partners?" Asks, "What did you realize about your community?" **Think** Teacher guides students toward further exploration with question, "Is there anything you can do about it?" Teacher extends student thinking with a "So what?" response. Teacher asks how to "showcase" the good things with the question, "How does a company sell a product?" "How could you 'sell' AP to others?" **Act** Teacher lists good things suggested by students on the chalkboard; highlights their favorite places (within walking distance of school).	**Look** Students recall and express orally recollections from previous summer's project. Students express their ideas about their community. **Think** Students recall from interviews from previous project that how people see their community affects how they feel about it. Students discuss places and activities in the community. Students explain how these show some good things in the community. Students connect to advertisements in newspapers, on TV. Students explore ways to "showcase" their community by creating a commercial. **Act** Students identify places, events, and so on, and identify those choices of places that comply with walking distance.	Questioning (Pre-assessment)— Students make connections to previous experience and feelings toward community condition.

Phase 2   Development

Materials: Videotaped TV commercials, easel pad, Internet access, school library, poster board, index cards, construction paper, scissors, glue, yarn, markers, pens, pencils, rulers, yardstick, specific props for each group commercial, five video cameras and film for each

Objectives/ outcomes	Teacher instruction	Student learning	Assessment
Students will: Identify topic, task, and audience. After reviewing gathered information, students will determine need for further information. Select and organize relevant information from varied print and nonprint formats. Utilize a graphic organizer to structure presentation.	**Look** Teacher guides students through the viewing and analysis of two taped commercials using List–Group–Label strategy. Preservice teachers (PTs) interview individual student partners about favorite place/location. Following individual interviews, form commercial groups. PTs guide students in information gathering using KWHL strategy to find out what they know, want to know, and where to find information. **Think** PTs guide students to review what they have learned from research. **Act** PTs focus students' attention on writing the script for their commercial. They use a storyboard for structuring the commercial, organizing information, and determining tasks to be accomplished. PTs guide students in determining their audience and the purpose for the commercial. PTs coach students in presentation skills. PTs and school personnel assist students in filming commercials onsite.	**Look** Students list characteristics, group-like characteristics, and label each group, creating categories. Commercial group members share lists and reach consensus on topic for commercial. Students gather information from sources. **Think** Students review gathered information. Determine if they need more information. Ask, "What do we do with the information?" **Act** Students determine tasks for each person in group. Students identify audience and verbalize the purpose for their commercial. Students practice acting out script. Students have say and agree on a successful take.	KWHL—Using this strategy organizes information students have gathered, raises questions they have, and requires identifying possible sources for information and summing up what they have learned. Storyboards—A concrete visual aid for students. PTs to lay out commercial, noting gaps, and so on.

Phase 3   Exploration

Materials: Location and setup for presentation, LCD projector or VCR			
Objectives/ outcomes	*Teacher instruction*	*Student learning*	*Assessment*
Students will: Review accomplishments and assess commercial and group project. Self-assess their learning.	**Look** PTs guide students in review of what they have done in the five meetings. **Think** PTs ask students to critique own commercials utilizing varied rubrics. PTs engage student partners in self-assessment of their own learning using open-ended questions. **Act** School principal, PTs arrange for an invited audience to view students' commercials.	**Look** Students discuss in their commercial groups what they have accomplished in five meetings with the PTs. **Think** Student commercial groups will create a list of what they liked and what could be improved. Students reflect on their own learning. **Act** Students introduce and show project to invited audience of peers, school personnel, parents, and community members. Students invite audience to participate in discussion following presentations.	Verbal group assessment of the five meetings while PT records their recollections. Use of rubric (open-ended questions, Likert scale, strength and areas for improvement lists) to critique commercial and project. Students self-assess own learning using open-ended questions, sentence starters, KWHL, List–Group–Label, Likert scales, checklists, and interviews.

REFLECTIONS ON THE LESSON

INTRODUCTION

During a summer session, preservice teachers (PTs) partnered with fourth- and sixth-grade students from an urban charter school. The school was located in a community that was in the beginning stages of urban renewal. In the process, the PTs learned that the students were dissatisfied with the condition of their community and wanted to do something about it—to make a difference in their community.

The following summer, PTs enrolled in the same course were partnered with the same students who were now fifth and seventh graders. Building on their desire to make a difference in their community, I suggested to the PTs that they work with the students to identify a project that they could share with the community about their community. The action research model served to guide the PTs through a planning process that allowed them to complete successfully every facet of the project. The PTs designed lesson plans for each meeting utilizing the Look–Think–Act learning cycle format in which they incorporated what they were learning in the course.

EXPLORATION

Look

At the first meeting, each PT was matched with one or two students. I asked questions of the students to refresh their memories of the previous summer's project and outcome: "What do you remember from last summer's project with your college partners?" Responses included the fun they had; recollections of the interviews with community members and their publication, *Aston Point Then and Now;* and their writings and illustrations, which sit on the school's library shelf. The students also recalled their expressing dissatisfaction with the condition of their community.

Think

The continuing questions guided the students toward further exploration of their discontent. I asked, "Is there anything you can do about it?" As the students thought about this, they remembered that one of the police officers who they had interviewed as part of last summer's project had said that improving the community begins in your own yard, keeping it and the space in front of your house clean and neat. One student remarked, "Yeah, we tried that here at school—cleaning up around our school and down the block. It just gets dirty again—people don't care." I responded to his statement with another question, "How might you get people to care?" A student volunteered, "To make people feel proud of where they live, of the community." I continued to question, "How might you do that?" Another student responded, "What's good in our community—look at the good things!"

TEACHER THINK-ALOUD

When I talked with the principal about this project, she remarked how appropriate the topic was as a continuation of the curricular unit on the community. The nature of the project addressed a social studies standard that pertains to extending students' knowledge of their community, including important places and buildings. In addition, it allowed them to reflect on what they learned about their community from the previous summer's project, specifically from sources like Web sites and their interviews with community people.

They talked about some of their favorite places and activities the community offers. At this point, I asked the students, "So what about them? What do these mean to other community members?" Further discussion among the students led to how they could "showcase" the good in the community, what the community has to offer. I offered some direction with this question, "How does someone sell a product?" Answers flew, "Advertisements in the newspaper, on TV! We can advertise our community on TV!"

Act

Finally the students agreed on the making of commercials to highlight favorite locations within walking distance of their school.

Look: Asking questions to activate previous knowledge

Think: Process and reflect

Act: Determine the project

DEVELOPMENT

In preparation for subsequent meetings with the students, the PTs with their peer group members designed lesson plans for the creation of the commercial during course class time. They identified learning strategies that were applicable for their students' identification of a topic and gathering information (LOOK), determination of how to proceed with the information (THINK), and writing and acting out of the script and filming of the commercial (ACT) while, simultaneously, identifying specific state standards that were being addressed.

TEACHER THINK-ALOUD

The PTs were amazed with how many standards could be addressed in all five language arts literacy areas—reading, writing, speaking, listening, and viewing.

EXPANSION

Look

Upon returning to the school, each of the groups reviewed what they had done with the PTs during the five meetings. The PTs organized their information by recording the activities of each day as the students related them.

Think

The first half hour of the sixth and final meeting was devoted to reflection. Each group was asked to play back its commercial and critique it by identifying its strengths and areas that could be improved. The PTs asked their students to reflect individually on what they had learned from this project. If you were to do it again, what might you do differently? The assessments took the form of open-ended questions, sentence starters, KWHL charts, List–Group–Label strategies, Likert scales, checklists, and interviews.

Act

The final products, the videotaped commercials, were shown to an audience made up of the students' peers, other grade levels, school personnel, and interested parents and community members. The students, with the aid of the school principal, invited the audience to ask questions and engage in discussion.

NEW JERSEY CORE CURRICULUM CONTENT STANDARDS, GRADES 5 AND 7: COMMERCIAL LESSON

EXPLORATION

Language Arts Literacy

3.1 Reading

    5 E. Reading Strategies

        1. Activate prior knowledge and anticipate what will be read or heard.

Social Studies

6.4.8 U.S. and NJ History

    A. Family and Community Life (Reinforce indicators from previous grade levels).

        6.4.4 A6. Describe situations in which people from diverse backgrounds work together to solve common problems.

DEVELOPMENT

Social Studies

6.4.4A Family and Community Life

A.4 Discuss the history of their community including the origins of its name, groups and individuals who lived there, and access to important places and buildings in the community.

Language Arts Literacy

3.1 Reading

3.1.7G Comprehension Skills

2. Distinguish between essential and nonessential information.

3.1.5H Inquiry and Research

3. Use multiple sources to locate information relevant to research questions.

7. Summarize and organize information by taking notes, outlining ideas, and/or making charts.

8. Produce projects and reports, using visuals, media, and/or technology to show learning and support the learning of an audience.

3.1.7H Inquiry and Research

1. Produce written and oral work that demonstrates comprehension of informational materials.

4. Self-select materials appropriately related to a research project.

3.2 Writing

3.2.5A Writing as a Process

5. Use strategies such as graphic organizers and outlines to elaborate and organize ideas for writing.

3.2.5, 7D Writing Forms, Audiences, and Purposes

1. Write for different purposes.

2. Gather select, and organize information appropriate to a topic, task, and audience.

3.3 Speaking

3.3.5A Discussion

2. Stay focused on a topic and ask relevant questions.

3. Accept others' opinions and respond appropriately.

5. Participate in class discussions appropriately. (also 3.3.7A 7)

3.3.7A Discussion

4. Define group roles using consensus to ensure task is understood and completed.

3.3.5B Questioning and Contributing

5. Solve a problem or understand a task through group cooperation. (also 3.3.7B 4)

3.3.7B Questioning and Contributing

2. Question to clarify others' opinions.

3. Integrate relevant information regarding issues and problems from group discussions and interviews for reports, issues, projects, debates, and oral presentations.

3.3.5D Oral Presentations

4. Use props effectively while speaking.

5. Maintain audience interest during formal presentations incorporating adequate volume, proper pacing, and clear enunciation.

7. Use verbal and nonverbal elements of delivery to maintain audience focus.

3.3.7D Oral Presentations

2. Use visual aids, media, and/or technology to support oral communication.

6. Develop speaking techniques, including voice modulation, inflection, tempo, enunciation, and eye contact for effective presentation.

3.4 Listening

3.4.5A Active Listening

2. Listen attentively and critically to a variety of speakers.

6. Listen to determine a speaker's purpose, attitude, and perspective.

3.4.7A Active Listening

2. Demonstrate active listening by analyzing information, ideas, and opinions to determine relevancy.

3.4.5B Listening Comprehension

1, 2, 3. Demonstrate competence in active listening through responding to a story, interview, or oral report, by interpreting and applying received information, and by asking questions, taking notes, and drawing conclusions on information presented.

3.4.7B Listening Comprehension

3. Critique information heard or viewed.

4. Critique oral presentations using agreed-upon criteria for evaluation.

3.5 Viewing

3.5.5A Constructing Meaning

4. Identify the target audience for a particular story, program, or advertisement.

3.5.7A Constructing Meaning

3. Analyze and respond to visual and print messages and recognize how words, sounds, and still or moving images are used in each medium to convey the intended messages.

3.5.5B Visual and Verbal Messages

3. Interpret verbal and nonverbal messages reflected in personal interactions with others.

EXPANSION

Literacy Language Arts

3.3 Speaking

3.3.5B Questioning and Contributing

5. Reflect and evaluate information learned as result of the inquiry.

3.4 Listening

3.4.5A Active Listening

7. Use when appropriate criteria/rubric to evaluate oral presentations, such as purpose, delivery techniques, content, visual aids, body language, and facial expressions. (also 3.4.7A 6)

CASE EXAMPLE A.3: ENVIRONMENTAL DECISION MAKING

This lesson demonstrates how the inclusion of different types of activities enables students to move systematically through the phases of a lesson. In the process they accomplish the diverse outcomes indicated in the state standards.

The lesson demonstrates the different types of activity Mr. W, the teacher, uses to initiate and facilitate student learning throughout the lesson. The Look–Think–Act sequence assists him in tracking the progress of the lesson, focusing separately on activities through which students acquire information, analyze or process that information, and engage in an action to either practice or demonstrate what they have learned.

Although students are Looking, Thinking, and Acting throughout, different phases of the lesson are identified as LOOK to denote a focus on students acquiring information, THINK to indicate that students are centered on processing or analyzing information, and ACT to signify "hands-on" student activity.

The commentary at the end of the lesson resulted from a formal review of the lesson, and presents how the teacher described and interpreted the lesson. The Teacher Think-Alouds represent teacher reflections of specific aspects of the lesson that were particularly significant to the teacher, a special application of the "Think" element of inquiry.

Subject: Environmental Science

Grade: 11/12

Unit: Environmental Decision Making

Topic: Citizens' Involvement in Local Environmental Concerns

Duration: 2 Weeks

New Jersey State Standards
Social Studies
6.2 Civics
12 D Citizenship 5

Language Arts Literacy
3.1 Reading
12 H Inquiry and Research 1, 3, 4, 5, 6
3.3 Speaking
12 A Discussion 1
12 D Oral Presentation 6
3.4 Listening
12 B Listening and Comprehension 1

Science
5.1 Scientific Processes
12 A Habits of Mind 3
5.10 Environmental Science
12 A Natural Systems and Interactions
12 B Human Interactions and Impact 2

(Continued)

(Continued)

The full list of standards is presented at the end of the lesson.

Materials: Community master plan map and chalkboard

Accommodations/Modifications: One-on-one instruction if necessary; peer tutors; provide step-by-step instructions; have appropriate reading materials; check on progress regularly; have an aide and assistive technology if possible; work with a special educator to modify instruction.

Bilingual English Language Learner Strategies: Peer tutors; labels in student(s)' language; word walls in native tongue and English; adapted texts; instructions and directions in representative/native language if possible; utilization of visuals such as pictorial schematics, graphic organizers, charts to illustrate concepts, directions, and so on

---

Phase 1   Exploration

Objectives/ outcomes	Teacher instruction	Student learning	Assessment
Students will: Explain how citizens' participation influences public policy. Identify environmental issues that impact their community. Demonstrate ability to work collaboratively in small groups.	**Look** The teacher will use a community master plan map as a way to focus students' attention and ask questions to prompt students to think about and discuss: • The environmental significance of preserved open spaces • A "Planned Unit Development" • The differing perspectives on how land should be used and who makes those decisions	**Look** Students discuss what they know about: • Identified preserved open spaces • Planned Unit Development • How decisions about land use are made	Teacher will pre-assess and activate student knowledge on topic.
	Think The teacher will ask students to partner with another student and to list other environmental issues in addition to land use that impact their community to share with class.	**Think** Student partners list issues and share with class. Students finalize list by combining like topics and eliminating those they determined are not environmental issues.	

	The teacher records all topics on chart paper.		
	The teacher asks students:	Students collectively discuss problems they recognize associated with the issues, and to help solve the problems, they would need to study the issue in order to explore solutions.	
	"What problems do you associate with the issues you have identified?		
	How can you help to solve the problems?"		
	Act	**Act**	
	Divides students into groups of 3–5 based on students' requested topics.	Students list three topics of interest and submit to teacher.	

Phase 2   Development

Materials: Library access for print and nonprint resources, Internet access			
Objectives/ outcomes	*Teacher instruction*	*Student learning*	*Assessment*
Students will: Identify and read a variety of appropriate sources for information on topic. Critically analyze gathered information. Identify differing perspectives on environmental issues.	**Look** Ask student groups to devise a plan for the study of their selected topic/issue. Teacher observes group progress and offers assistance as needed. **Think** Teacher asks student groups to adjust concept maps to reflect new knowledge. Suggest they agree on a method of reporting to the class about their topic.	**Look** Each student group commences construction of a concept map. They first identify key concepts and possible print and nonprint sources for gathering information. Students arrange for interviews with contacts at state and local agencies. **Think** Following information gathering, students critically analyze information to determine relevance, further questions, need for more information, and differing perspectives presented concerning issue. They make adjustments to concept map to accommodate new knowledge.	Assessment will be based on quality and characteristics of Group Concept Maps.

(Continued)

Phase 2 (Continued)

Objectives/ outcomes	Teacher instruction	Student learning	Assessment
Communicate clearly knowledge and understanding of an issue.		Students agree on an appropriate method for reporting and assign tasks for the presentation.	
Demonstrate active listening by assessing peers' presentations.	**Act** Teacher assists students to construct an assessment tool for assessing each group's presentation. Teacher assesses presentations.	**Act** Students and teacher construct an assessment tool for assessing each group's presentation. Student groups present their findings on their environmental issue to class members. Peers assess presentations.	Use assessment tool for teacher/peer assessment (Summative).

Phase 3 Expansion

Materials: Assessment tools, Quick Write handouts			
Objectives/ outcomes	Teacher instruction	Student learning	Assessment
Students will:	**Look**	**Look**	Quick Write
Reflect on own understanding of issues through self-assessment, and teacher and peer assessments.	Teacher asks student groups to review and evaluate the process and final presentations with aid of assessments, identifying their strengths and areas for improvement.	Students utilize assessments to review and evaluate process and final presentations and identify their strengths and areas for improvement.	
Construct plan for presentation to community.	**Think** Teacher asks students to do a Quick Write to capture essence of each topic presented.	**Think** Students complete Quick Write.	

Objectives/outcomes	Teacher instruction	Student learning	Assessment
	Teacher asks students to reflect on what they have learned about having a voice concerning decision making in their community.	Students engage in reflective discussion about what it means to have a voice in decision making in their community.	
	Act	**Act**	
	Teacher asks students how they can be proactive with the information learned from their studies.	Student groups explore ways for informing the community about what they have learned from their environmental issue studies.	
	Teacher asks each environmental group to prepare a plan that includes the rationale, the identified audience, and an outline of the presentation and the format to be used.	Students in each group construct a plan to communicate the findings of their environmental study to an identified community audience.	Community Presentation Plan

REFLECTIONS ON THE LESSON

EXPLORATION

Look

TEACHER THINK-ALOUD

I decided to begin the course in environmental science with a unit on environmental decision making oriented toward my students' community that is located on the Atlantic Ocean. Making it relevant to their interests, both individually and collectively, drew them into the course content immediately. By using their own experiences, they were better able to understand how the interdependent components of the environment are affected by human activity and natural phenomena, a science standard for environmental studies. By using a map as a visual reference and questions, I guided my students toward connecting to what they already knew about environmental issues, who is involved in making decisions concerning issues, the gravity of the outcomes, and the relevance to the local community. My goal is for my students to realize as citizens, they have both a responsibility to their community and a voice in the decisions made about their community, addressing a social studies standard concerning the rights, responsibilities, and roles of citizens.

Using a community master plan map as a prompt, Mr. W questions students about specific areas on the map as a way to focus their attention, develop interest, connect to what they know, and introduce them to the beginning lesson of the course. As students identify the parks and other preserved open space, Mr. W lists them on the chalkboard. One student, noting the designation of a dog-walking beach as a "Planned Unit Development," asks, "What does this mean?" Mr. W poses the question to the class. After much discussion among the class members, they come to the conclusion that this natural area in a predominantly residential town was spared from development. Mr. W asks, "Who made this decision?" Students determine that it would be up to the people who live in the community. Mr. W continues, "Would all the people be in favor of this proposed plan?" The students decide there would be people who may not be in favor of it. Mr. W asks, "Who?" and lists students' suggestions of those who might be opposed to the use of the land for a dog-walking beach. The ensuing discussion focuses on looking at the potential for differing perspectives on how the land might have been used.

Think

Mr. W asks the students to make a list with a partner of other environmental issues in addition to land development that are currently affecting their community. As the students share their topics, Mr. W records them on chart paper. The students revise the list, combining related topics or eliminating those that do not fit the criteria. To engage students in a discussion about the issues they identified, Mr. W asks, "What problems do you associate with the issues you have identified? How can you help to solve the problems?" Students collectively discuss problems associated with the issues, and to help solve the problems, they would need to study the issue to be better informed about the issues and how to deal with them. This process actively involves students in identifying environmental topics, revising the list, and selecting topics of interest to study.

Act

Once satisfied with the topics, students list their top three choices and submit them to Mr. W, who then sorts them into groups of three to five based on their preferences.

DEVELOPMENT

Look

TEACHER THINK-ALOUD

The use of the concept map serves as a collaborative organizational tool for each student group to collectively outline its study. Also, it allows me to monitor at a glance the progress being made in each group and to offer assistance as needed.

Each group charts its own understanding of its topic with the aid of a group-constructed concept map. Once the group members decide the important concepts related to their topic, they identify possible print and nonprint sources they could use for gathering information, such as newspaper articles, books, pamphlets from pertinent agencies, interviews with relevant people, and Internet sites. Mr. W circulates, observing the progress of the group concept maps and offering assistance as needed.

Think

After gathering the information, the students determine relevance to their topic, additional questions they have, a need for more information, and indication of differing perspectives. They adjust the concept map to accommodate the new knowledge and/or changes in their original plan. Mr. W asks how they would like to share what they have learned to inform class members of the environmental issues affecting their community. Each group decides on an appropriate method for reporting what they have learned to their peer audience and assigns tasks to each group member. In preparation for the presentations, Mr. W and the students collaboratively construct a rubric that will serve to assess the variety of methods selected for the group presentations. They carefully identify the performance criteria, revisiting the learner outcomes for the lesson to guide them and identifying any additional criteria the lesson addressed.

Act

Student groups present their findings on their environmental issue to class members. Their peers and the teacher assess the presentations.

EXPANSION

Look

Mr. W gives each group its assessment from peers and the teacher. He asks the students to review the process they went through to prepare their presentation and to reflect on the presentation itself to identify the strengths and the areas needing improvement.

Following the group's self-evaluation, he asks them to consider what they have learned from the activity and what they might do differently.

Think

At this point, Mr. W asks the students to do a Quick Write as a formative assessment to analyze and synthesize the information they have gleaned from each presentation. He gives each student a paper divided into sections and labeled with each of the groups' environmental topics. This activity allows students to review in writing and then orally what they have been learning about environmental issues, the role of community members, and the consideration of differing perspectives, and to raise unanswered questions they have.

Act

Finally, Mr. W poses the question of how they can be proactive with the information learned from their studies. The students explore and discuss ways of sharing what they have learned with other students and different groups in the community.

Each environmental group prepares a plan that includes the rationale, the identified audience, and an outline of the presentation and the format to be used. The plan provides another summative assessment that will include self-assessment as well as teacher assessment.

TEACHER THINK-ALOUD

By incorporating formative assessments as progress checks and a review of the summative assessment, my students had multiple opportunities for reflection on their own learning.

NEW JERSEY CORE CURRICULUM CONTENT STANDARDS: ENVIRONMENTAL DECISION MAKING LESSON

SCIENCE

5.1.12 Habits of Mind

A.3 Engage in collaboration, peer review, and accurate reporting of findings.

5.10.12 Environmental Science

A.1 Distinguish naturally occurring processes from those believed to have been modified by human interaction or activity: climate change, ozone production, erosion and deposition, threatened and endangered species.

B.2 Use scientific, economic, and other data to assess environmental risks and benefits associated with societal activity.

SOCIAL STUDIES

6.1.12 Social Studies Skills

A.2 Formulate questions and hypotheses from multiple perspectives, using multiple sources.

A.6 Apply problem-solving skills to national, state, or local issues and propose reasoned solutions.

6.2.12 Civics

D.5 Discuss how citizens can participate in the political process at the local, state, or national level, and analyze how these forms of political participation influence public policy.

LANGUAGE ARTS AND LITERACY

3.1.12 Reading

H.1 Select appropriate electronic media for research and evaluate the quality of the information received.

H.3 Develop increased ability to critically select works to support a research topic.

H.4 Read and critically analyze a variety of works, including books and other print materials about one issue or topic, or books by a single author or in one genre, and produce evidence of reading.

H.5 Apply information gained from several sources or books on a single topic or by a single author to foster an argument, draw conclusions, or advance a position.

H.6 Critique the validity and logic of arguments advanced in public documents, their appeal to various audiences, and the extent to which they anticipate and address reader concerns.

3.3.12 Speaking

A.1 Support a position integrating multiple perspectives.

D.6 Use a rubric to self-assess and improve oral presentations.

3.4.12 Listening

B.1 Listen to summarize, make judgments, and evaluate.

References

Aldridge, J., & Goldman, R. (2007). *Current issues and trends in education* (2nd ed.). Boston: Allyn & Bacon.

Anderson, L. W., & Krathwohl, D. R. (Eds.). (2001). *A taxonomy for learning, teaching and assessing: A revision of Bloom's Taxonomy of educational objectives* (Complete ed.). New York: Longman.

Appiah, K. A. (2006). *Cosmopolitanism: Ethnics in a world of strangers.* New York: Norton.

Atweh, B., & Burton, L. (1995). Students as researchers: Rationale and critique. *British Educational Research Journal, 21*(5), 561–575.

Atweh, B., Christensen, C., & Dornan, L. (1998). Students as action researchers: Partnerships for social justice. In B. Atweh, S. Kemmis, & P. Weeks (Eds.), *Action research in practice: Partnership for social justice in education* (pp. 114–138). London: Routledge.

Baldwin, S. (1996). High school students' participation in action research: An ongoing learning process. In E. Stringer, M-F. Agnello, S. Baldwin, L. Christensen, D. Henry, K. Henry, et al. (Eds.), *Community-based ethnography: Breaking traditional boundaries of research, teaching and learning* (pp. 132–146). Mahwah, NJ: Lawrence Erlbaum.

Bandura, A. (1965). Influence of model's reinforcement contingencies on the acquisition of imitative responses. *Journal of Personality and Social Psychology, 1*, 589–595.

Bandura, A. (1986). *Social foundations of thought and action: A social cognitive theory.* Englewood Cliffs, NJ: Prentice Hall.

Berliner, D., & Biddle, B. (1996). *The manufactured crisis: Myths, fraud, and the attack on American schools.* Reading, MA: Addison-Wesley Publishing.

Bloom, B., & Krathwohl, D. (1956). *Taxonomy of educational objectives. Handbook 1: The cognitive domain.* New York: David McKay.

Bruner, J. (1966). *Toward a theory of instruction.* Cambridge, MA: Belknap Press.

Caine, R. N., & Caine, G. (2006). The way we learn. *Educational Leadership, 64*(1), 50–54.

Caldwell, J., Huitt, W., & French, V. (1981). *Research-based classroom modifications for improving student engaged time.* In D. Helms, A. Graeber, J. Caldwell, & W. Huitt (Eds.), *Basic skills instructional improvement program: Leader's guide for student engaged time.* Philadelphia: Research for Better Schools.

Carr, W., & Kemmis, S. (1986). *Becoming critical: Education, knowledge and action research.* London: Falmer.

Christensen, L. M., Stubblefield, E., & Watson, G. (2008). Building a sense of history: Folk art for early childhood learners. *Social Justice Feature, Social Studies Research and Practice* (online journal www.socstrp.org/) 3(1).

Coleman, J., (1966). *Equality of educational opportunity*. Washington, DC: U.S. Government Printing Office.

DeVries, R., & Kohlberg, L. (1987). *Constructivist early education: Overview and comparison with other programs*. Washington, DC: NAEYC.

Dewey, J. (1933). *How we think: A restatement of the relation of reflective thinking to the educative process* (Rev. ed.). Boston: Heath. (Original work published 1909)

Dewey, J. (1938). *Experience and education*. New York: Macmillan Publishing Company.

Dewey, J. (1964). The relation of theory to practice in education. In R. D. Archambault (Ed.), *John Dewey on education* (pp. 313–338). Chicago: University of Chicago Press.

Eisner, E. W. (1987). *Cognition and curriculum*. New York: Longman.

Eisner, E. W. (1997). *Enlightened eye: Qualitative inquiry and the enhancement of educational practice* (2nd ed.). New York: Merrill Publishing Company.

Elkind, D. (1995). School and family in the postmodern world. *Phi Delta Kappan, 76,* 8–14.

Freire, P. (1970). *Pedagogy of the oppressed*. New York: Herder and Herder.

Friere, P. (2000). *Pedagogy of freedom: Ethics, democracy, and civic courage*. Lanham, MD: Rowman & Littlefield Publishers.

Gallagher, J. M., & Reid, D. K. (2002). *The learning theory of Piaget and Inhelder*. New York: Authors Choice Press.

Gardner, H. (1999). *Intelligence reframed: Multiple intelligences for the 21st century*. New York: Basic Books.

Gardner, H. (2006). *Multiple intelligences: New horizons, the development and education of the mind*. New York: Basic Books.

Goals 2000: Educate America Act of 1994, Pub. L. No. 103-227, (1994).

Goodman, Y. (1978). Kidwatching: An alternative to testing. *National Elementary Principal, 57,* 41–45.

Greene, M. (1995). *Releasing the imagination: Essays on education, the arts, and social change*. San Francisco: Jossey-Bass.

Harrow, A. (1972). *A taxonomy of the psychomotor domain. A guide for developing behavioural objectives*. New York: David McKay.

Huitt, W. (2003). *A transactional model of the teaching/learning process*. Valdosta, GA: Valdosta State University, Educational Psychology Interactive. Retrieved June 7, 2007, from http://chiron.valdosta.edu/whuitt/materials/tchlrnmd.html

Hunter, M. (December 1990/January 1991). Hunter lesson design helps achieve the goals of science instruction. *Educational Leadership, 48*(4), 79–81.

Jencks, C. (1972). *Inequality: A reassessment of the effect of family and schooling in America*. New York: Harper and Row.

Kincheloe, J. L. (2001). *Getting beyond the facts: Teaching social studies/social sciences in the twenty-first century* (2nd ed.). New York: Peter Lang.

Kincheloe, J. (2005). *Critical pedagogy primer*. New York: Peter Lang.

Kincheloe, J. L., Slattery, P., & Steinberg, S. R. (2000). *Contextualizing teaching: Introduction to education and educational foundations.* New York: Addison, Wesley & Longman.

Krathwohl, D., Bloom, B., & Masia, B. (1964). *Taxonomy of educational objectives: Handbook II: Affective domain.* New York: David McKay.

Loewen, J. W. (1999). *Lies across America: What our historic sites get wrong.* New York: The New Press.

Malaguzzi, L. (1994). Listening to children. *Young Children, 49*(5), 55.

McLaren, P. (2006). *Life in schools: An introduction to critical pedagogy in the foundations of education* (5th ed.). New York: Allyn & Bacon.

Mezirow, J. (1991). *Transformative dimensions of adult learning and fostering critical reflection in adulthood: A guide to transformative and emancipatory learning.* Hoboken, NJ: Jossey-Bass.

National Commission on Excellence in Education. (1983). *A nation at risk: The imperative for educational reform.* Washington, DC: U.S. Department of Education.

New Jersey Department of Education. (2004). *The New Jersey core curriculum content standards.* Trenton: State of New Jersey Department of Education.

No Child Left Behind Act of 2001, Pub. L. No. 107-110, 115 Stat. 1425 (2002).

Nussbaum, M. C. (1997). *Cultivating humanity: A classical defense of reform in liberal education.* Cambridge, MA: Harvard University Press.

Piaget, J. (1973). *To understand is to invent: The future of education.* New York: Grossman.

Piaget, J., & Inhelder, B. (1973). *Memory and intelligence.* New York: Basic Books.

Pinar, W., & Reynolds, W. (1992). *Understanding curriculum as phenomenological and deconstructed text.* New York: Teachers College Press.

Rosenshine, B. (1995). Advances in research on instruction. *Journal of Educational Research, 88*(5), 261–268.

Schon, D. (1983). *The reflective practitioner.* New York: Basic Books.

Slavin, R. (2006). *Educational psychology* (8th ed.). Boston: Pearson/Allyn & Bacon.

Spradley, J. P. (1980). *Participant observation.* Orlando, FL: Harcourt Brace Jovanovich.

Stiggins, R. (2002). Assessment crisis: The absence of assessment FOR learning. *Phi Delta Kappan, 80*(10), 758–765.

Stiggins, R., Arter, J., & Chappuis, J. (2007). *Classroom assessment for student learning.* Princeton, NJ: Educational Testing Service.

Stringer, E. (2007). *Action research* (3rd ed.). Thousand Oaks, CA: Sage.

Stringer, E. (2008). *Action research in education* (2nd ed.). Upper Saddle River, NJ: Pearson.

Sunal, C. S., & Haas, M. E. (2008). *Social studies for the elementary and middle grades: A constructivist approach.* Boston: Allyn & Bacon.

Vygotsky, L .S. (1962). *Thought and language.* Cambridge: MIT Press.

Vygotsky, L. (1978). *Mind and society.* Cambridge, MA: Harvard University Press.

Index

About the Authors

Ernest T. Stringer, PhD, spent his early career as a primary teacher and school principal and later was lecturer in education at Curtin University of Technology in Western Australia. From the mid-1980s, based at Curtin's Centre for Aboriginal Studies, he worked collaboratively with Aboriginal staff and community people to develop a wide variety of innovative and highly successful education and community development programs and services. His work with government departments, community-based agencies, business corporations, and local governments assisted them to work more effectively with Aboriginal people. In recent years, as visiting professor at the University of New Mexico and Texas A&M University, he taught research methods courses and engaged in projects with African American and Hispanic community and neighborhood groups. As a UNICEF consultant, he recently engaged in a major project to increase parent participation in the schools in East Timor. He is author of the texts *Action Research* (2007), *Action Research in Education* (2008), *Action Research in Health* (with Bill Genat, 2004), and *Action Research in Human Services* (with Rosalie Dwyer, 2005). He is a member of the editorial board of the Action Research Journal and past president of the Action Learning and Action Research Association (ALARA).

Lois McFadyen Christensen, PhD, is an associate professor in the Department of Curriculum and Instruction at the University of Alabama at Birmingham. She is an elementary social studies specialist at the undergraduate and graduate levels teaching undergraduate, master's, and doctoral level course work. For 6 years, she facilitated a collaborative, cross-disciplined approach on the Birmingham civil rights movement. Dr. Christensen's publications and presentations are often in conjunction with inservice teachers and pertain to social studies research, critical pedagogy, and the Reggio Emilia approach to early childhood education.

Shelia C. Baldwin, PhD, has an education career spanning 27 years, with 17 years in public school and 10 in higher education. As a high school teacher of English, reading, and ESL, she taught diverse students who were often struggling and disengaged, which inspired her to eventually pursue her PhD. Her early work in action research with high school students to study the cultural diversity in their environment was transformational in her perception of classroom life. Her interest, promoting collaboration between teachers and students in the exploration and implementation of alternative instructional approaches, has been a focal point in her continuing work and research as a teacher educator. She has examined her own classes to learn more about teacher candidates' developing theories about teaching, students, and learning environments. She has developed and supervised service learning field experiences in urban settings for undergraduate and graduate teacher candidates in content literacy courses to provide them with autonomous experiences in diverse settings. Her integration of action research processes introduces the concept of teacher as researcher and guides them toward critical reflection on their experiences that contribute toward their developing theories. She has developed a master's level action research course for both initial certification candidates and practitioners.

Supporting researchers for more than 40 years

Research methods have always been at the core of SAGE's publishing program. Founder Sara Miller McCune published SAGE's first methods book, *Public Policy Evaluation*, in 1970. Soon after, she launched the *Quantitative Applications in the Social Sciences* series—affectionately known as the "little green books." Always at the forefront of developing and supporting new approaches in methods, SAGE published early groundbreaking texts and journals in the fields of qualitative methods and evaluation.

Today, more than 40 years and two million little green books later, SAGE continues to push the boundaries with a growing list of more than 1,200 research methods books, journals, and reference works across the social, behavioral, and health sciences. Its imprints—Pine Forge Press, home of innovative textbooks in sociology, and Corwin, publisher of PreK–12 resources for teachers and administrators—broaden SAGE's range of offerings in methods. SAGE further extended its impact in 2008 when it acquired CQ Press and its best-selling and highly respected political science research methods list.

From qualitative, quantitative, and mixed methods to evaluation, SAGE is the essential resource for academics and practitioners looking for the latest methods by leading scholars.

For more information, visit **www.sagepub.com**.